PROFITABLE PLANS

7 STEPS TO A FINANCIALLY SUCCESSFUL BUSINESS

FEMKE HOGEMA

ISBN: 9789493231252 (ebook)
ISBN: 9789493231245 (paperback)

Cover: Femke Hogema, picture by Bart Honingh

Copyright © Femke Hogema, 2021

Publisher: Amsterdam Publishers

info@amsterdampublishers.com

TESTIMONIALS

Femke has proven herself time and time again as an expert serving entrepreneurs. Profitable Plans is yet another brilliant resource she has created and provided to entrepreneurs to make their dreams a reality, thereby serving her mission. If you are an entrepreneur, this is a must read. Do yourself a huge favour and listen to what Femke is telling you in this book. Don't just read it, follow through on the action items she gives you - you won't look back! - **Lisa Campbell, CPB, CPFP-Mastery & Canada's Profit Coach**

Femke has reinvented the goal setting process and turned it into easy to follow process that keeps owners focused on their goals while knowing before they even start if the goals will make them more profitable. Profitable Plans is a great easy to follow action guide on how to improve your business.

Profitable Plans gave me a way to clearly breakdown the steps I need to take to hit my financial goals within a timeframe that works for me. Budgeting is something most of us don't like to do even though we think it's something that would help out business. Budgeting seems very prehistoric now that I have learned Profitable Plans. It was easy to follow and easy to implement and now I have something way better than a budget. I have a plan that can help me be profitable. - **John D Briggs, CPA Partner Incite Tax, USA**

If entrepreneurs do not reach their goals, it rarely happens on the "home stretch". Reaching goals has everything to do with how entrepreneurs are setting them.

Goals are screwed up at the start, not in the final stage. Entrepreneurs need a plan that sets them up for success from the very first step. That's where most plans fall short.

Profitable Plans is the one truly comprehensive guide that fills that exact need. A must-read for any entrepreneur who wants something to show for their hard work when they cross the finishing line. - **Benita Königbauer, Head of Profit First Professionals Germany**

Everybody needs a copy of Profitable Plans if they want to run a successful business. Femke breaks down each of the mindset, plan and action themes within the book and sets up the reader to take action, easily. I highly recommend it. Don't just read it, share it as every business should be profitable! - **Laura Elkaslassy, Adroit Business Solutions, Australia**

Permanent profitability is attained when mindset, aligned business model and a clear vision are married together. Femke Hogema nails this trifecta in Profitable Plans with the perfect balance of entertaining stories, strategy and clear actions steps. - **Amber Dugger, Founder of Profit for Keeps™, USA**

CONTENTS

For Hans, my father,

because you have always been my greatest supporter.

FOREWORD

For many entrepreneurs, owning your own business means freedom. Finally, you can work where, when and how you want to. And, usually, entrepreneurs don't want to do things just for the money. They really want to contribute something with their service or product, sometimes even make the world a better place.

Being free *and* making a contribution. Who wouldn't want that? But there's a flip side to the story. A harsh reality. Because a lot of entrepreneurs aren't free at all. They're constantly stressed about money and can barely make ends meet. Or their earnings are "okay," but not nearly enough to make all their dreams come true.

Real freedom requires profit. Your business needs money like your body needs oxygen. Money, just like oxygen, has to flow. And if there's a shortage, everything shuts down. But – and here comes a big *but* – making a profit and earning money aren't usually a top priority for entrepreneurs. Money isn't a goal for them, but only a means. Money is a logical result of doing the right things. But that's not how the game is played. That's not how entrepreneurship works. Entrepreneurship also requires you to take the financial side of business seriously. A company is only viable if it's profitable, and being responsible for its profitability is your task as the entrepreneur.

If you want to be a successful entrepreneur, if you want to make your dreams come true, you'd better learn to like money. Dare to earn money, and make it a goal (maybe not the only goal, but at least one of them). And make a serious, realistic and executable plan that shows you what you need to do to make money. And, finally, take action. Every day, take the right actions to realize your goals. Mindset. Plan. Action. That's it.

In this book, I give you practical tools to make your own profitable plan. I do this with a personal approach. I share my thoughts, my successes and my failures. I also use real examples from entrepreneurs. Everything is aimed at motivating you to make your own plan, so that you get as much as possible out of it!

With my help, hundreds of entrepreneurs have made their own profitable plans over the past six years. "Why on Earth didn't I do this sooner?" is something I hear often. Making your plan delivers immediate insight, and ensures that in the weeks and months to come, you make the right choices and make more profit. It's that simple.

Don't wait any longer. Make your plan and go change the world.

Femke Hogema

PREFACE

What makes some entrepreneurs successful and others not? It's an intriguing question, and one that I've thought about for years. Why does Tony Robbins have multiple million-dollar businesses and a happy marriage, while other entrepreneurs have to conclude after three years that they have failed: their business doesn't generate enough money to be viable and, on top of that, their personal life has suffered because of all the hours they've been working. Is it luck? The right knowledge? Hard work? The right connections? Or, it is a bit of all those things, but mainly something else? I think it's the latter. For sure, I believe you need a bit of luck and have to work pretty hard to create a successful business. However, more than anything, success requires the right mindset, having a good profitable plan and acting consistently.

Mindset. Plan. Action. Just three simple words. But these three words make all the difference between struggling in the margins and financial success.

Your mindset, what you believe in, defines what you do and, therefore, what you achieve. If I believe this book will never be a success, I'm not focused on promoting it. It would be a waste of energy. A book that isn't promoted will never get very high on the bestseller lists. On the other hand, if I believe this book has the potential to be #1 on the best-seller list, then I'll do everything to ensure it reaches the top. This way, the chance it does actually reach #1 is much bigger. But you might know what I'm going to say next: the risk of failure also increases. Because if this book doesn't make the top-10, I've already gone out on a limb with this paragraph.[1]

What you believe, therefore, defines what you achieve. If you want a financially successful business, it requires a different mindset than if you only want to make ends meet every month. That's why, in the first chapter of this book, I give you the tools to manage your mindset.

However, you won't succeed with *only* a fantastic mindset. The second step is a plan: a good, realistic and profitable plan. Without a plan, you'll drift along on an ocean of possibilities. Your plan gives you clarity in what, when and to whom you want to sell, how much turnover you'll generate, what costs you need to incur, and how much will be left over. Your plan tells you what you've got to do in order to generate the turnover, and which marketing and sales actions you consistently need to take. You create your own road to success. In Chapters 3-6, I give you the practical tools to make your own plans.

Do you have the right mindset and a solid plan? Then, you just need to carry out your plan. Do the work, and you'll succeed. It sounds simple, but if it were that easy, everyone would do it! It sounds crazy, but just doing what you need to do isn't that simple. We get distracted, we're not focused, or there's too much on our plate to enable us to do what we need to do. And, as contradictory as this sounds, I suspect you know exactly what I mean. In the final chapter of this book, I share a great model for you to use, to make sure you really do get down to doing what's needed to create your own success.

Mindset. Plan. Action. These are the themes throughout this book...the book with which you can create your own success.

---

1. Note on the English translation: The Dutch version of this book indeed became a #1 national bestseller and stayed in that position for over a month.

1

CREATE THE RIGHT MONEY MINDSET

* * *

Whether you think you can, or you think you can't - you're right – Henry Ford

* * *

One afternoon in the summer that I turned 17, I came home after a day out shopping in Arnhem, the city closest to my hometown in The Netherlands. "I've changed my mind," I said to my parents. "I've decided that I'm not going to study social work. I'm going to study business administration instead." My parents were in shock, especially my mother. She taught social work and my father was a director at a children's home. Logically, I was to follow in their footsteps. I had registered for the social work program just months before. Working with troubled kids had seemed the right thing for me. Now I came home announcing I was changing my path to something they knew nothing about.

"What?" and "why?" were their first questions. I told them how that afternoon while on the bus on the way home, I'd passed a large, stately building in Arnhem. "Higher Economic Administration Education" could be seen in large letters on the stone façade, and at that very moment, I knew where I wanted to study. I was always a fan of money. As a teenager, I kept a detailed description of all my expenses. On vacations I saved my extra pocket money (because according to my father everything was twice as expensive in France) in order to be able to exchange a big pile of French francs for Dutch guilders when we got home three weeks later. I was fascinated by my father's second-hand bicycle hobby. I always wanted to know exactly how much he made on the bikes that he sold to others in our town and how much he had spent on the parts needed to fix them up. Even at a young age, I loved the clarity of money, the insights it gave. I felt in my bones that I wanted to understand how the financial world worked and that my future was there.

This is where my journey began. On this journey I'm inspiring entrepreneurs to create a business that's financially healthy and profitable. To improve their relationship with money. Because, whatever your mission – helping others, improving the world, eradicating diseases – your business needs to be financially healthy, so you can truly fulfil your mission in the world. Making a profit is essential.

Profit conjures up all sorts of images for entrepreneurs: desire and pleasure, but also resistance and even anger. "But it's not about the money!" or "I shouldn't earn more than I need" are often the reactions I get when I suggest that making a profit is an essential part of running a business. Or entrepreneurs claim, "As long as I'm doing what I'm good at, the money will come in by itself!"

Of course, there's some truth in those statements. Because they're right: money isn't the most important thing in the world. Love, health and happiness are far more important than money. And of course, passion is a key aspect of being an entrepreneur. Passion is a driving force behind any successful business.

But that's not the whole picture. It's not a question of either/or; you need both. Quite simply, making a profit is simply essential if you're an entrepreneur. No profit; no business.

Money Mindset

I understand where these beliefs come from. Because many of us heard from an early age that "money can't buy happiness," "you need to work hard for your money," "you shouldn't stand out from the crowd," or "rich people are stingy." We were told, "Don't think you can become something you're not." And, what's more, many women were taught that they'd be better off finding a wealthy husband than focusing on earning and it is the man's job to provide for his family, while the woman's place is to raise the children.

Just this past weekend while at a party, I listened in on a conversation between my husband and the father of a classmate of our youngest child. He is a young, emancipated father. Both he and his wife work and he picks their children up at school just as often as she does. Still when he heard that I earn more money than my husband, he laughingly said to my husband, "You married up!" I know for sure he would never have said the same to me if the situation were reversed. It is simply not "normal" for a wife to earn more than her husband.

We have all received messages about money, some positive, others negative. When we don't question these messages, they become beliefs: opinions we now consider truths. Perhaps some of these messages you got from your parents. They told you, "Do something creative, you're not very good at math." You believed that, and now that you are an entrepreneur, bookkeeping is a thorn in your side because "numbers aren't your thing." This kind of thinking is actually completely ridiculous. You have gotten where you are now because you have the capacity to learn new things, sometimes practically overnight. You can learn new things. You have learned new things.

Managing your finances is simply another thing you can learn. If you experience resistance to doing so, there is probably another reason than just your "trouble" with numbers. Financial success can be tempered by cultural norms. Being successful is not something to strive for in many European countries. In the Netherlands, you don't want to appear to be bragging; it is better to be seen as average. I've also spoken to colleagues abroad and they reported much the same. For example, in the Czech Republic, impacted by 40 years of communism, it may be unwise to stand out from the crowd. Also in Australia the tall poppy syndrome is prevalent; if you perform higher than the group they will tear you down and speak badly of you. And then quite some women report feeling as though there's always an underlying belief that they don't deserve to make money.

When I was 12, I was bullied at school for having the highest grades. When I was 16, I went to high school in the United States for a year. There I was on the Dean's List and my name was posted in the principal's office as one of the ten best students in the school. Suddenly I was allowed to be proud of my good grades. I wasn't bullied at all. My classmates looked up to me. I learned then (unconsciously) that I am allowed to be proud of my accomplishments and don't have to hide my success. Being successful was no longer dangerous. Rather, it was something to strive for.

1.1 Beliefs drive behavior

A belief is an idea that you have come to view as true. Beliefs can be supportive, such as "if someone else can do it, I can learn it as well" or "if I know what my goal is, I can create my own success." But beliefs can also work against you. Think about beliefs like "I can't do that," "I'm not worth it," or "I'm just not a good salesperson."

Beliefs are rooted deep within us. They often take shape during our childhood. Parents, teachers and other important people in our lives send – often unconsciously – messages. And if you hear something often enough, you end up believing it. A belief that has had years to nestle itself in our minds is difficult, but not impossible, to let go of. You just don't realize a belief is actually only an opinion you think is true at that moment.

The problem with beliefs is that they unconsciously influence our behavior. If you believe that dogs bite, you will act much differently when you run into one than if you believe that dogs are loyal friends. And be honest, what chance do you have of becoming a millionaire if you believe that rich people are stingy?

Beliefs end up proving themselves; they are self-fulfilling. I remember vividly how in elementary school we would all sing songs around the piano. The teacher apparently didn't think I sang very well, because she elbowed me and whispered, "You, just mouth the words!" What I heard was, "You can't sing!" This message had such impact on me that I only had to hear it once to believe it. For years, I believed that I couldn't carry a tune. If I had to sing (sometimes you have to, like when it is someone's birthday,) I did so full of anxiety and in a constricted, squeaky voice. Of course, that didn't sound very good and so my belief that I couldn't sing was repeatedly confirmed.

Years later in my twenties, I signed up for a dance workshop. I enjoyed dancing and was looking forward to three dance-filled days. When I arrived, I was horrified to discover that it was a sing and dance workshop. I must have not read the invitation very carefully and already the first morning I was confronted with the task to sing a solo within a group of four other attendees. By the end of those three days I didn't believe any more that I couldn't sing. I had a wonderful time and enjoyed singing together with the others and sang just as well as they did, which is just well enough. A few years later I joined a choir at work after encouragement from colleagues. We would rehearse every week and sang at the big annual company meeting. You can watch a compilation online at ProfitablePlans.com. I don't think that I will ever make a living from singing, but I learned it is something you can learn how to do. Even I could. "I can't sing" was something I believed because an authority figure, my teacher, sent me that unfortunate message at a vulnerable age.

Exactly the same principle applies to entrepreneurship. Let's look at two web designers who create websites of basically the same quality. Both designers promise that with their websites you can attract new clients more easily. Designer A believes the websites he builds are not really better or worse than those of his competitors. He views websites as a commodity and thinks there really isn't much differentiation among them. Designer B believes that the sites he develops for his customers are special. Through his unique approach to marketing and technology his clients will earn significantly more with their new websites.

Who do you think asks a higher fee for his services? And will potential customers be willing to pay more for designer A or B? Exactly. The website designer will never earn more for his services than he believes they are worth.

Whether you are a web designer, industrial engineer, coach, accountant or lawyer, what you believe your services are worth has a huge influence on how you present your services to others and, therefore, how much a customer is willing to pay. Ultimately, your beliefs dictate the profit you make.

For a long time, I didn't believe that becoming a millionaire was for me. About ten years ago, I remember participating in a Business Boot Camp. We were given the assignment to visualize ourselves as millionaires. I didn't do the task. At the time, "being rich" was so far from my reality that I could only look around in great surprise at the room full of people concentrating on millions of euros. I believed that becoming rich was for others. Now, many years later, I want to have financial freedom. I envision myself and my family in a spacious house in the countryside. My children study debt-free and we enjoy the freedom we created for ourselves.

Ten years ago, I worked for an hourly rate. If I wanted to earn more, I had to work more. I quickly reached the maximum that I could earn. Now I know that I could never achieve financial freedom that way. I don't work per hour anymore, but instead have developed a business model where my earnings are not dependent on my time. This model hasn't made me a millionaire yet, but I do believe that I will achieve financial freedom. The effect is that I act in the correct way in order to create financial freedom.

The change from believing "becoming rich is not for me" to "I create financial freedom for myself and my family" did not happen overnight. I worked on it. I started to manage my money mindset.

How much money do you believe you need? How does it feel to say to yourself out loud, "I am a millionaire?" Does it feel good? Or do you feel resistance? Realize this: there is no right or wrong, but what you believe has an enormous influence on what you do and what you eventually achieve.

1.2 Changing your beliefs

Beliefs drive behavior and your behavior determines your results. The basis for a successful company begins with thoughts of success. And the wonderful thing about thoughts is that you can control them.

Managing your money mindset and changing your beliefs begins with awareness. It is important that you are aware of and can identify your own beliefs. Ask yourself, "What do I believe about money?" and "What does being profitable mean to me?" Think about how money was discussed in the home where you grew up. What messages did you receive from your parents and at school about money? You could discover negative as well as positive messages.

I love making money. Years ago, it was hard for me to identify with becoming rich, but at the same time I certainly wasn't opposed to having money. My father sold second-hand bicycles. During the week, he was the director of a children's home and on the weekends he repaired bikes. It was a "hobby gone wild" and quite a lucrative one. I remember how on Sunday afternoons he would pull a large wad of money out of his back pocket and count it on the kitchen table. He clearly enjoyed counting his money. I was unconsciously learning that money can bring pleasure and there is nothing wrong with having it. This belief plays an essential role in the work I do.

If your beliefs about money stand in the way of what you want to achieve, it is time to change them. And this is possible. You weren't born with your beliefs; they developed over the years. You can consciously choose to believe something else, something that will help you to reach your goals.

You can change your beliefs in five steps:

1. Recognize your beliefs

Make a list of what you believe about money. What beliefs – positive and negative – do you have about money, earning money and making a profit? If you have difficulty, I created a list of 50 beliefs for inspiration, which you can download for free at ProfitablePlans.com.

2. Create understanding for the beliefs that hinder you

Recognizing your beliefs can be emotional. I recall a conversation with a client (I will call her Laura) about money and her money mindset. Laura told me that her mother gave her the message that rich people are selfish. She hadn't heard this once, but tens, hundreds of times. And she began to believe it. Therefore, becoming rich was something to avoid at all costs. It would mean she was one of the bad guys, especially in the eyes of her mother. When she realized that this belief was nothing more than that – a belief – she was in shock. I saw that Laura became angry with her mother, which was understandable, as Laura had denied herself the chance to earn more money based on a belief that turned out to be false.

Before I could work with Laura on finding a better, more supportive belief, it was essential that she understood why she believed what she did. I explained to her that her mother didn't know better. Most likely her mother had a negative experience with wealthy people and she wanted to protect Laura from a similar experience. Once Laura understood what was behind what her mother told her, there was room for her to change her belief.

If you notice that you become angry or sad upon recognizing beliefs that hinder you, it is important you understand where the belief came from and how you came to see it as truth. Realize that your parents or other important people in your life probably didn't know better. I believe that everyone makes the best choice they can at a particular moment. That in retrospect it was a mistake doesn't mean the intention was bad. The teacher at my elementary school probably just wanted the songs sung around the piano to sound beautiful. In principle there is nothing wrong with that intention, but a more thoughtful strategy would have been to teach me how to sing, rather than criticizing my untrained voice.

3. Challenge your beliefs

A belief is an opinion, thought or idea that you consider to be true. But that is actually the crux: it isn't necessarily, as a matter of fact, true. It is not a proven fact that rich people are stingy. Indeed, there is enough evidence to indicate the opposite is true. Bill Gates is an example of one of the world's wealthiest people. He has given away 50 billion dollars to charity. That's not peanuts! Even relative to his immense fortune of 100 billion, it is an impressive sum.

My belief that "becoming rich is not for me" was not an absolute truth. I had my own frame of reference; my family wasn't wealthy, but also not poor. I didn't have a role model. I didn't know any rich people. My belief was not so inexplicable, but that didn't make it true.

The third step in changing your beliefs is to challenge them. You do this by asking yourself, "Is this true?" "Can I really know that this is true?" "What evidence do I have that this is true?" "Are there examples that prove the opposite?"[1] Soon, you will start to doubt your own beliefs. Beliefs are not truths; they are opinions or ideas that you have adopted as truths. But if you examine them closer, you will always see that a different conclusion is also possible.

There is another important question to ask yourself: "Does this belief help me?" Now that you know your belief is not an absolute truth, but something you have come to accept as true, you can also choose to believe something else...even if the alternative isn't true either. I have believed for years that I am an excellent parallel parker, better than the average woman (wink, wink). And after many years of driving, I am pretty good at it. However, when I first started driving, it took me several attempts before my car was reasonably parked – just like everyone else. Undoubtedly someone once told me that I was good at parallel parking and after hearing it a couple of times, I believed it. Every time I deftly maneuvered my car into a tight spot, my belief was confirmed. And every time that it didn't go so well, I ignored it. I focused on the times it did go well. My belief helped me to become better at parallel parking.

Imagine what would have happened if when I just started driving, I had heard a few times, "You're helpless, get out of the car, I'll do it for you!" What do you think it would have done to my self-confidence? And how well does parallel parking go if you think you're hopeless at it? It doesn't really matter if what you believe is true. What is more important is that you understand that what you believe drives your behavior and therefore affects the outcome. That means you can choose to believe in something that will help you reach your goals.

**The only thing that's keeping you
from getting what you want
is the story you keep telling yourself**
Tony Robbins

4. Formulate new, supportive thoughts

Now that you have gotten to know and better understand your existing beliefs and thoughts about money and finances and have introduced doubt as to their absolute truth, it is time to formulate new, supportive thoughts. Ask yourself the following question: "Which thoughts – that I don't believe yet but could be true – could help me reach my goals?"

There are a few essential elements in this question:

- *You don't have to believe it yet* – you believed something else for years. It's not strange that you don't have faith in the new idea...yet.
- *As long as it helps you reach your goals* – As soon as a new thought makes you happy, it is an improvement. Ask yourself, "If I believe this, will it help me reach my goals?" This is true for any goal: financial success, peace of mind, happiness.
- *There isn't only one positive alternative for your negative belief* – If your hindering thought is "rich people are selfish," your new belief could be "rich people are generous." However, instead of just using the opposite, you can also formulate a completely new idea. For example, "because I am rich, I can help more people." The point isn't to find the perfect new thought, but to find a positive thought that makes you happy and will help you achieve your goals.

Your new thought must meet two important conditions:

1. *Positive formulation* – It is important that your new thought is formulated positively. A thought such as "rich people are not selfish" is the opposite of "rich people are selfish," but you can feel that the energy is pretty much the same. It's not a thought that makes you happy. And to be honest, the thought "rich people are not selfish" doesn't really provide

direction. It won't help me reach my goals. The point is that the negative word "selfish" is still there. Our brains don't hear the word "not." Don't think of a pink elephant! What is the first thing that comes to mind? Exactly. It is essential that you formulate what you do want and not what you don't want.

2. *As if now* – In addition to being positive, formulate your new thought in the present tense, as if it is already true. "I want to become rich" is less powerful than "I am rich." Wanting something is much less powerful than being something. You can train your brain to believe that you are already rich. You can *want* to be rich until your dying day, but wanting alone won't help you achieve it.

5. Integrate your new thought into your daily life

Formulating a new thought is wonderful and gives you a lot of energy. But it will really bear fruit when you start believing it and when after time it feels more real than the old belief that held you back. When your new, supportive belief really starts working for you and influencing your daily actions, you can achieve your goals and dreams.

Since I decided I would have financial freedom, it is a regularly recurring topic of conversation between my husband and me. When we are going through our busy agendas having trouble trying to arrange something, he always asks, "When are you going to earn enough for me to quit my job?" And I always reply, "I'm working on it!" We have had this exchange countless times. To begin with it felt like a little joke, but after a while we started to believe it. Now it is a promise.

How will my new belief actually help me to achieve results, you may ask yourself? If I look at myself, I can name several concrete actions and results that materialized once I started to believe in my financial freedom. I actively explored a better revenue model for my business. My husband and I talked with a financial planner about our financial future, and I started saving more money for our retirement. I also took a course in investing. It was not the right course, so I'm not there yet, but I'm taking steps in the right direction. But I think the most important thing is now I have the courage to earn more money. Next to my old belief, "becoming rich is not for me," there was another familiar belief that was an obstacle to my goal. That was the thought "we have more than enough," which makes it impossible to become rich. I would feel guilty for every additional euro in my bank account. Now that I believe in financial freedom for my family and me, every extra euro is helping bring me closer to my goal.

Action Steps

1. Recognize your beliefs about money. What do you believe about money? Which messages did you receive about money? Take a look at the free list of 50 money-related beliefs which you can use to gain insight into your own: ProfitablePlans.com.
2. Create understanding for your beliefs.
3. Challenge your beliefs.
4. Formulate new, supportive thoughts.
5. Integrate your new thoughts.

In this chapter, I gave you a five-step model to create a money mindset that will allow you to achieve your goals. In the next chapter, we will work on your mission and vision. Why do you do what you do, and where are you going?

---

1. Byron Katie, *Loving What Is: Four Questions That Can Change Your Life.*

2

WORK FROM YOUR DRIVE

* * *

**There is a powerful driving force inside every human being
that, once unleashed, can make any vision, dream or desire a
reality – Tony Robbins**

* * *

Before I was born, my parents had twins, two boys. They were born
10 weeks prematurely. Nowadays, such premature babies usually
survive, but in 1974 that was unfortunately not the case. The boys
died within a day of their birth. The support my parents received
after such a great loss was much different than it would be today.
They were sent home and told to forget the twins as soon as
possible, and that was that. I was born a year later in 1975. Surely
due to all his unprocessed emotions, my father unconsciously
decided then and there that I was "the one." I was the perfect
daughter.

I gladly wore the badge of perfect daughter. I did everything I could
to avoid disappointing my father. I did my best at school, got good

grades, went to college, got a good job, wrote a book and was on TV. I went on to write more books and appear on TV again and again, but sadly he isn't here any longer to witness my success.

I won't deny it was difficult for me to carry the burden of my father's expectations. But at the same time, I learned a valid lesson: that I am responsible for my own success – and more importantly – I can create my own success.

I consider success (in whatever form) to be a responsibility. I received the gift of life; the twins did not. Because of this, I feel a great responsibility to fulfill my potential, to ensure my life is meaningful and to make the most of it. Not that I experience being successful as difficult now. I have done a lot of soul-searching and know better every day how to make my own choices. I truly enjoy and am sincerely inspired by the things I do.

I believe that everyone can achieve what they want. Success is not a coincidence. Success occurs when you make a mission-based plan and act consistently to make that plan a reality. Success is not reserved only for a chosen few. Everyone can create their own success – whatever success means to you – because everyone can decide success in their own terms.

Making the most of life is our purpose. I don't believe in just being satisfied with what you have or hoping things will get better. I believe in standing up for what you want and making it happen. Today. Tomorrow. Every day. Sharing this belief and inspiring, challenging and motivating you to create your own success – that is *my* mission.

I create my own success. Without an inner drive I would not have succeeded. Without my drive, my courses, books and seminars would be empty words without a soul. There's a big chance you bought this book because you feel my drive and it inspired you.

Mission and vision: what drives you?

Do you know what gets you out of bed every morning, even when it's hard? What your higher purpose is? Your ultimate goal? Your business' driving force? Why you do what you do and where you want to go?

Your mission and vision provide a firm foundation and direction for your company. Without a foundation your message is empty and inauthentic. Without direction you are adrift on the ocean of opportunities, but don't get where you want to be. It is important to determine your mission and vision and then starting working from there.

2.1 Mission: why do you do what you do?

Your mission is your "why," the reason your company exists. It is about what is important to you, your identity, what you believe in and why you do what you do. Your mission gives what you do meaning.

In addition to wanting more freedom or more money, the majority of entrepreneurs start their companies with a higher purpose in mind; there is something very important to them that they want to realize. In my case, I want all entrepreneurs to have financially healthy and profitable businesses. Perhaps you couldn't realize your purpose working for someone else, and that is why you decided to start your own business.

Everyone knows the story of the salesperson who claims to be able to sell ice to an Eskimo. They mean they can sell anyone anything, regardless of whether their customer needs or wants it. I'd rather buy something from someone so genuinely passionate about their service or product that their eyes light up when they tell you about it (and not just because they have the opportunity to make a sale). Those are the people I believe. By talking with them, I feel more and more connected to the solution that they offer. I start to believe they can help me and that I have already taken the first important step towards finding the answer to my problem.

Someone whose mission is crystal clear is Anne Quaars. Anne is a Dutch marketing and communication strategist. It is her mission to challenge female entrepreneurs to not only think big, but to *do* big. She wants them to quit hovering on the sidelines with their "hobbies," earning extra "pocket money." She wants them to be ambitious, set serious prices and speak up. "Big, Bold & Brave," is her motto. Because Anne communicates her mission so powerfully, you know exactly who she is and what she does. If you aren't interested in big business, then don't call her. This way she only attracts her ideal clients and they know exactly where to find her. The rest are filtered out.

If you follow Anne on social media, you can see this effect in the reactions to her posts. Some adore her (hearts and stars galore) and others abhor her and think she's rude, biased and over-the-top There's no middle ground! 😉

Maybe your mission is clear to you. Maybe it has a prominent place on your website and in all your marketing messages. Great! If it is clear what you stand for, potential clients can choose you for the right reasons. The more explicit you are, the easier it is for the customer.

Find your mission

Your "why" is there. You don't need to create it. You just need to find it. The best way to find your "why" is to ask yourself a series of questions:[1]

1. Why do you do what you do?
2. Why is _____ important? (Fill in the gap with the answer you gave to question 1)
3. Why is _____ important? (Fill in the gap with the answer you gave to question 2)

4. Why is _____ important? (Fill in the gap with the answer you gave to question 3)
5. Why is _____ important? (Fill in the gap with the answer you gave to question 4)

Sometimes you need to continue to ask "why" four or five times, sometimes seven times. It can help to switch between asking "Why is _____ important?" and "What's the benefit of _____?" and "What does _____ mean to you?" These questions can provide new insights. Take your time and trust that you already know the answer. You don't need to make something up.

You can ask yourself these questions or have someone else ask you. In any case, take the time and space you need. Shut off your phone and turn off your email or go for a walk. The advantage to getting someone to ask you these questions is that the answers often come to you quicker than when you ask yourself. Additionally, the other person can write down your answers and sometimes ask the question just a bit differently which helps you get to your "why" easier. Look for someone who you know can limit themselves to just asking the questions. It is counterproductive when they help you answer the questions or re-formulate or re-interpret your answers in some way.

I've worked out my own mission for you as an example:

Question	Answer
1. Why do you do what you do?	I want to help entrepreneurs have financially sound and profitable businesses.
2. Why is that important?	Because otherwise a business can't exist.
3. Why is it important that a business continues to exist?	Only then can one be successful.
4. Why is it important to be successful?	To live up to my full potential.
5. Why is it important to live up to your full potential?	Because I was given the gift of life.

Boom. The moment I knew my mission, it was magical. All the puzzle pieces fit together. You'll see that the final answer is not the one that I have on my website. It is too personal, but I do share the other answers. However, knowing the "ultimate why" of my mission is very valuable.

Working from your mission

Discovering your mission is fantastic. You feel purpose in everything you do, and if you don't feel that way, it's often a signal you're doing the wrong things. While discovering your mission is a very important milestone, you haven't reached the finish line yet.

How do you ensure that you are working from your mission? That your mission is tangible in everything you do, for you as well as your customers? That you aren't just checking items off a to-do list and making money?

Keep your mission alive

Does this sound familiar? You were at a course or workshop and you completed a self-reflection or other exercise and you felt deeply connected to your mission, but a few days later during a difficult negotiation with a potential client your mission is about the furthest thing from your mind? You know it is not enough to feel connected to your mission a few times a year, so how do you keep your mission alive? It is important that you constantly remind yourself of your mission for a few months. Just like you put in your agenda that you need to go to the gym three times a week, otherwise you "forget" to go, keeping your mission alive is something you have to actively *do*. For example, print your mission out and hang it up in your office. Remind yourself every day why you do what you do. It is good to change your mission poster every few weeks, give it a different color or font, otherwise you get used to it and don't notice it anymore.

I remind myself of my mission when I meditate. I literally visualize my ideal clients and what I contribute to their lives. I've also taught myself to always reconnect with my mission right before key moments. Right before I go on stage or start a webinar, I remind myself why I do what I do. Believe me, this works.

Don't be afraid of other people's opinions

As soon as you stand up for what you believe, other people will have an opinion about it. There is a common Dutch saying and while it doesn't translate very well, the meaning is clear: if you raise your head above ground level (i.e. above everyone else), it'll get chopped off! In the Netherlands we learn at a young age not to strive to be better than others; being average is just fine. But if you believe that, you won't be successful. In my opinion, you can only be a success if you decide to stand up for what you really want and accept all the consequences.

People will judge. And not only the trolls on social media, but also your friends and family. Brush yourself off, smile and keep standing proud. If you are on the receiving end of a lot of feedback, you know you have touched a nerve and should see this as confirmation that you are on the right track!

Communicate from your mission

Communicating from your mission with your team, customers and other stakeholders is essential. If you really start a conversation with your mission in mind, it can be very emotional. I often get tears in my eyes when I talk about how important I think it is for entrepreneurs to have financially healthy and profitable businesses. That is because I truly believe it and always feel the connection to the deepest layer of my mission. They aren't empty words, but words that come from my soul.

Experiment with a new way of introducing yourself at network events or other occasions where you are in the spotlight. Don't tell people your profession – "I'm a coach/bookkeeper/lawyer"— but tell them *why* you do what you do. Your conversations will have much more depth. People will get a feeling for what you stand for and will be eager to hear what you actually do!

2.2 Vision: where are you going?

Your vision is more concrete than your mission. Your vision is about what you want to achieve long-term with your company, based on your "why." It is the future, an ambitious goal, focused on what you want to contribute to the world. Your vision is also your compass. Thanks to your vision you always have a way to check if you are on the right path.

A vision may be grand, ambitious and even a bit unattainable or vague. A vision doesn't have to be static, but can change over the years. A vision can be just one sentence or a whole paragraph. There can be various aspects of your long-term goal in it. Think about what a business owner wants to achieve for the staff, the customer, the environment and what that means for the company's finances.

A clear vision provides you with the tools you need to make the right choices to steer your company in the right direction at any moment. A vision is inspiring. You know why you are doing what you are doing, and that energizes and motivates you and your team to work together towards the same goal. Without vision you are drifting along aimlessly. Your team loses motivation and underperforms. Your potential clients get confused about what you do and go elsewhere.

For example, my vision is: by training Profit advisors through my courses, books and seminars I inspire entrepreneurs worldwide to build financially sound and profitable businesses. In 15 years, 70% of all entrepreneurs will know Profit First.[2]

Develop your vision

For some entrepreneurs, their vision is crystal clear and might even be prominently displayed on their website. Other entrepreneurs used to have one, but it's somehow gotten lost over the years. And others have never had a vision. If you don't know your vision like the back of your hand, and you feel it is time for your business' next step – more profits, better customers, more time or whatever – go through the following steps yourself or with your team:

1. Start from your mission

Connect with your mission. Through the perspective of your mission, look at the world around you 10 or 20 years from now. How does the world look if you are living your mission? What do you want to have achieved by then?

2. Explore the developments

Look at the developments in your field. What trends are there and how important are these trends for your vision? What opportunities are there and how can use make use of these? What threats are there and how will you deal with them? What changes do you notice in your customers' needs? By exploring how your area of business is evolving you will get more insight into where you want to go.

3. Make choices

When you think about your vision it is inevitable that you will have to make some hard choices. You can only go in one direction. By choosing your ultimate goal, you are excluding other possibilities.

4. Formulate your vision concisely, powerfully and attractively

It is important that your vision is formulated concisely and powerfully and that it creates interest. Hearing or reading your vision should give you, your team and other stakeholders a "YES" feeling. Pay attention to these conditions when formulating your vision:

1. *Positively formulated*- avoid words like "not" and "none," and instead say what you *do* want. For example, for a bookkeeping business, "We use the most modern technologies" instead of "We are not a receipt-factory."
2. *As if it is already true* – Avoid words like "want," "maybe,"

and "possibly." Act like it is already true: "We are an organization that….," instead of "We want to be an organization that…"

3. *Ambitious* – Your vision can be larger-than-life and ambitious. In your vision, you can indicate how many people you want to inspire, what geographical area you want to reach, and how much turnover you want to achieve. A vision that misses ambition is boring. People shrug and go on with their day. When a vision has ambition, it is inspiring. People take a moment to think about what it means for them. An ambitious vision drives results. "All entrepreneurs in the Netherlands" is more motivating than "entrepreneurs."

4. *Specific for your business* - While your vision can be a little vague and unattainable, it is important that it is relevant to your business and not too general. Once your vision is clearly specific to your company, your team members will remember it and integrate it in their work and potential clients will be inspired.

5. *Focused on the future* – It is clear that a vision is about what isn't there yet; it is something to work towards. This can be expressed by using a year, "2040," or number of years, "in twenty years," in your vision.

Communicate your vision

Just like your mission, your vision deserves a prominent place in your communication. Don't hesitate to share your vision in conversation, at network events, on your website, in your brochures, during interviews and internal meetings. Particularly the latter is often forgotten. If you think, "My team already knows all that," your vision won't live among the team members. If they aren't regularly reminded of the vision, it will soon be forgotten. The team will become demotivated and won't work toward what you really want to achieve. If they no longer have the ultimate goal in mind, they'll make bad choices. They won't have the ambition needed to work a little harder. Communicate your vision so often it becomes part of every fiber of your business. Then every action at every moment will be driven from the same guiding force.

Action steps

Connect with your mission and formulate your vision. Are your mission and vision already clear to you? Then check whether you are always working and communicating from your driving force and if you can improve. If your mission and vision aren't clear for you yet, free up half a day to work on it. Grab your agenda now. If you don't plan it, it won't happen.

In this chapter I have given you the tools to connect with your mission and formulate your vision. Your mission and vision form the basis from which you work. If your foundation wobbles, so will everything else. In Chapter 3, you will work on your customer's real problem and what you offer to solve it.

---

1. This is also known as the 'Five Times Why' method and is attributed to Sakichi Toyoda, who used it to detect problems within the production process at Toyota.
2. Profit First is the most practical, accessible and fun method I know for entrepreneurs to manage their cashflow. Profit First is a worldwide system. Check profitfirstprofessionals.com (USA), ProfitFirstProfessionals.nl (Netherlands), profitfirstaustralia.com.au (Australia), profitfirstpro-fessionals.ca (Canada), www.profit-first.de (Germany)

3

SOLVE YOUR IDEAL CLIENT'S REAL PROBLEM

* * *

Sell the problem you solve, not the product – Source unknown

* * *

At the end of 2006 I had had enough. I worked for Accenture as a Financial Manager for a large client. I led a financial department of 12 people and generally had the freedom to work as a stand-alone shop within a big company. I was content – until the disastrous day in the fall of 2006 when I unexpectedly got a new manager. My new boss had a particularly hierarchical style. He came in and completely took over. My ideas were no longer important; I had to do what was expected. One day I expressed my frustration with the situation. I said, "I have the feeling that there isn't any possibility to do things my way. I wonder if you even listen to me." He said these infamous words to me, "Of course I listen to you, but you still need to just do what I tell you." I resigned and registered my company at the Chamber of Commerce on February 22, 2007.

Dissatisfaction with being an employee was what motivated me to start my own business. I was looking for freedom to think and do what I wanted. What was your reason to start your business? According to the Dutch Central Statistics Agency, two-thirds of entrepreneurs start a business for positive reasons such as wanting to be their own boss and organize their own time. A quarter also has negative incentives together with the positive, like being laid off or not being able to find a suitable job. Ten percent start a business because they see it as the only option they have.

So, you can say that most entrepreneurs start businesses for personal reasons. Business-oriented reasons, like finding a gap in the market or having a new solution for an existing problem, aren't mentioned as a primary motivator. If you think about it, the business-oriented reasons should absolutely factor into the decision to start a new company.

In my opinion, a business is a driven and profitable organization that sells a solution for the ideal client's real problem and delivers it in the most efficient way possible. There are nine elements to this definition. I will go through them with you:

1. *Driven* – A driven organization is one with drive, a vision and a mission. I discussed this in the previous chapter.

2. *Profitable* – No profit, no business. Profit is necessary for the continuity of the organization.

3. *Organization* – An organization is the total of people, systems and processes. As long as *you* are the business and it is completely dependent on your time, energy and ideas, all activity will grind to a halt if you are sick, on vacation or too old to work. This means there is no continuity.[1]

4. *Real problem* – You add value when you have an answer to your customer's real question. Only then can you run a successful business.

5. *Ideal customer* – If you help everyone with everything, no one will be interested in your product. Only when you really understand who can benefit the most from your service or product can you reach out to them, and only then will they pay attention.

6. *Solution* – Once you understand what your ideal customer's problem is, you can find a solution. Ideally, the solution shouldn't only be reliant on your efforts, but is developed by the whole organization – the people, systems and processes.

7. *Sells* – The solution to the problem needs to be sold before it can be delivered. This means that the entrepreneur needs a good marketing and sales strategy.

8. *Delivers* – Only once the solution is delivered has the entrepreneur met his or her obligation. Quality and customer satisfaction are important elements in how a product or service is delivered.

9. *Efficient* – The organization must deliver the solution as efficiently as possible. This means that you use the fewest possible resources like time, money and effort to achieve the most results. You only have a profitable business when the income is higher than the costs in time, money and effort. This element will be addressed extensively in Chapter 5, "Create your Profitable Plan."

In this chapter, we are going to work on the following elements: problem, ideal client and solution.

3.1 What is the real problem?

Successful companies solve real problems. Consider Uber, which solved the problem of expensive taxis that are in short supply. You order an Uber with the app and usually within five minutes you're hopping in and are on your way! You pay automatically with your credit card; it can't be simpler! Uber was started in 2008 when two men, the founders, were stuck in Paris and couldn't find a taxi or public transportation. They ran into a real problem, which led to the birth of their business model.

Solutions for problems are everywhere. McDonald's discovered people like predictable, affordable food that they can get quickly without having to set foot in the kitchen. McDonald's was one of the first fast-food chains and in 2019 their revenue was more than 20 billion dollars.

The five important life areas

You don't always have to solve a problem to have a successful business. There is also an enormous market for fun things such as the theatre, home decoration or toys. If your company delivers services or products that don't actually solve a problem, ask yourself what value your product adds. To what question is your product the answer? Is it the need for relaxation? Status? Beauty? Health?

Whether your client has a problem (a backache) or a desire (to look beautiful), most of the issues people deal with can be categorized into one of the five life areas: security/safety, health, relationships, status/identity, spirituality/growth/meaning.

Security/safety

The need for security and safety is a basic need shared by every person. Having a place to live gives a sense of security, but so does having the right insurance, saving for retirement and having one's finances well organized.

Health

Health is a life area in which billions of dollars are spent. Think about the pharmaceutical and diet industries. But there are also many small companies that contribute to this area, sometimes without realizing it: a coach who helps you prevent a burn-out, the personal trainer who keeps you fit so you have more energy and less back pain, or the dietician that helps you to eat more nutritiously. These are all examples of entrepreneurs active in the area of meeting health needs.

Relationships

When you think of earning money with relationships, you often think of couples therapy. But I also believe the entertainment industry plays a big part in this area: going out to eat together, to a movie or a weekend away. Marketers use images of candlelight dinners and couples walking hand-in-hand through the woods. These businesses are all earning money in the area of relationships.

Status/identity

We are all people with egos, and any way you look at it our egos cost money. The car industry makes exceptionally good use of this life area. Nobody actually needs a car that costs more than 20,000 dollars. There are a lot of cars for under 20,000 dollars that will get you safely from point A to point B, but still cars that cost 50,000 dollars or more sell like hotcakes. They sell because they convey the image that we're successful. Status. I, too, bought a new car when I didn't really need one. Status. I drove an Opel Corsa for many years, and even though it still safely took me from point A to point B, I decided to buy a BMW1 just because I felt it suited me better.

The beauty and fashion industries, along with furniture and interior design stores play to our egos and desire for status. Maybe your business does as well? Are you a business coach who helps clients build businesses of 100,000 dollars or more? Hiring you as a coach might appeal to your client's sense of security, but for many people, it can't be separated from their sense of status and identity either.

Spirituality/growth/meaning

I live in a rich and safe country, and mostly likely you do, too. Discovering the meaning of life is gaining in importance for many us of in the most economically developed parts of the world.

According to Maslow's hierarchy of needs[2], you can only begin to think about life's meaning if you have enough food to eat, you're safe, have healthy intimate relationships and a general feeling of accomplishment. In less economically developed countries where having enough to eat is often a daily challenge, there isn't as much need for a business model built around self-fulfillment as there is in more economically developed ones. We gladly spend money on personal, emotional and spiritual development, on meditation courses, retreats and yoga. These all appeal to the desire for spiritual fulfillment.

To which of your customer's questions does your service or product provide the answer? Are you selling a solution to their problem? Or have you focused mostly on the product you offer, rather than the true needs of your customers?

Strategic mistakes

Two things often go wrong in entrepreneurs' strategies:

1. The real problem is not being solved, or

2. The entrepreneur solves a real problem, but he or she doesn't communicate this well, so the customer doesn't realize the entrepreneur is offering the solution.

Passion is not enough

Small or new entrepreneurs too often think from their own perspective instead of the client's. The entrepreneur has a skill, talent, or area of expertise, and they build their service or product around that passion. Don't get me wrong; having passion for your product is essential. People buy from people and preferably from enthusiastic people. I already discussed this in the previous chapter. But passion, knowledge or skills is not enough. We all know entrepreneurs who can't give their wonderful "whatever" away, simply because no one needs it.

Sell solutions for problems and not products

Then there are the entrepreneurs who do actually have a solution to a real problem, but don't talk about the problem in their marketing, so the customer has no idea that he or she needs the product. Think about EMDR (Eye Movement Desensitization and Reprocessing) training. EMDR is a very effective method to work through traumatic experiences. But if your website only says you offer EMDR, and your ideal, traumatized client doesn't know what EMDR is, then she or he will never find your website and will never become your client. So, don't sell products – sell solutions to problems.

When I became an entrepreneur in 2007, in addition to the temporary work I did, I offered financial courses. My course "Reading financial statements for the self-employed" was not selling. My ideal client had no interest in learning how to read financial statements. Only many (many, many) years later did I discover that not being able to read these statements was not my clients' problem. Their problem was that they would lie awake at night worried about whether they could pay their taxes and that they weren't able to make the right choices to make their businesses successful. Once I started selling products that solved those problems, my courses were sold out.

I've sold my best-selling online training course, "Calculate how much taxes you owe in 10 minutes" (for Dutch solopreneurs), almost a thousand times. This course offers a wonderful solution for a really big problem. Many self-employed people have no idea how much in taxes they have to pay. It keeps them up at night. In only 10 minutes and for only 50 euros, my course offers them a super concrete solution - and it sells like hotcakes.

Interview your best customer

How do you find out what the real problems of potential clients are? You have lots of options: be active on social media in relevant groups, talk to people at network events and see what colleagues in your field do, listen to podcasts, read blogs, etc. But by far the best way to find out which of your client's problems you can solve is to ask. Talk to your customers. Start with your very best, most satisfied customers and ask them if they'd be willing to free up 15 minutes of their time to talk to you. Explain that you want to improve your service and that you want to talk to your best customers. Your client will be honored to be considered one of your best customers and most people just love to talk, particularly about themselves and their needs. My experience is that you will be able to interview quite a few people without any problem. Among other things, ask them the following questions:

1. Why did you decide to purchase my service or product?

With this question, you ask about the underlying problem. You want to capture the client's words very precisely. Because if you hear those words back from others, then those are *the words* that resonate with your customers. Once you have those words, you can and should use them in your marketing communications.

1a. What problem did my service or product offer a solution to? If you don't get a good answer to question 1, question 1a can help the customer to be more specific.

2. Why was it important for you to solve the problem mentioned?

The answer to this question gives you insight into the customer's deeper motivations. Often these are associated with one of the life areas mentioned previously: security/safety, health, relationships, status/identity, spirituality/growth/meaning. Insight into this is very valuable. I could have referred to my successful online course," Taxes for the Self-employed in 10 minutes," as a "fiscal training." I did not. Instead, I brought in the life area of health. I didn't talk about my clients' lack of fiscal knowledge, but I conjured up a solution to their sleepless nights and anxiety.

3. How did my product help solve your problem?

This answer will provide insight into exactly how your product or your service is of benefit to them.

4. What are you most satisfied with in our collaboration?

Your customer will not only mention what you or your company are doing well, but also what is important to him or her and what he or she might want more of. If your customer says they are really happy with your personal approach, you could emphasize that even more in your communications, which will really set you apart.

5. What frustrates you with my industry?

It's very valuable to understand what you're not doing right or what's wrong with your product or service, so you can improve. That's why you want to ask your customer to look critically at your product. But chances are your customer will be reluctant to be completely honest with you about your service or product. Instead, if you ask about the problems in the education, internet or marketing industry – whatever industry you work in – your customer will feel much freer to honestly tell you what is bothering them. You might discover there is an opportunity you have been missing, an opportunity where there is a real problem for you to solve!

It is very important that you write down everything your client says. It's even better to record it, so that you can make a transcript later. These are your marketing messages! Only when you use the words of your ideal customer will other ideal customers recognize themselves and their needs in your communications. Many website and marketing texts are written from the perspective of the entrepreneur, and because he or she is an expert in the problem that they solve, the words used are usually far removed from the customer experience. Think of the bookkeeper's website that promises to deliver an "IFRS-compliant annual statement." What entrepreneur would ever use those terms? And who is attracted to this statement? If the bookkeeper had gotten to know his customer better, he would have probably promised "no hassle with the tax authorities" or something similar. Consider the website developer who offers Search Engine Optimization. Is that what entrepreneurs talk about with each other when their websites can't be found easily online? Or do they say, "When I search on Google, my website doesn't come up." Shouldn't the web designer promise "better search results on Google?"

Ask for a testimonial

An in-depth interview with your customer can provide wonderful statements about your business... so good that you might want to make a testimonial out of them. Just ask! The in-depth interview shouldn't be a sneaky way to get a testimonial out of a client, but there's nothing wrong with saying at the end of the conversation, "I am so happy with all this useful information you've given me. I am so glad to hear that you are satisfied, and while it was not the original intention, would you be willing to provide me with a testimonial?"

If the customer agrees, which is usually the case, you have various options. You can have them actually write the testimonial based on several questions you provide them with, or you can write it yourself based on the interview and send it to them to review. Be sure to mention you'd like to include a photograph with the testimonial along with their name and company, and how you want to use the testimonial. If the customer prefers not to provide a testimonial, which is a possibility, let them know that is fine and that you are incredibly happy with the valuable information you got out of the interview and that it will really help you to improve your service or product.

3.2 Who is your ideal customer?

Besides knowing what your customer's real problem is, you also need to know who your ideal customer is. It is impossible to solve everything for everyone and likewise it is also impossible to focus your marketing on everyone.

Choose a niche

It is necessary to choose a niche, i.e. an ideal customer. It can be a customer from a specific industry, but you can also target customers of specific demographics - such as age, gender, family composition or income.

Customers want to work with experts

Many entrepreneurs claim to be able to solve everything for everyone. I remember speaking to a coach at a network meeting. I asked him, "What industry do you coach in?" He said, "It doesn't matter. Everything." I don't know how you see it, but his answer left me unsatisfied. It's like being in a restaurant and asking the waiter about the special of the day and he says, "Everything's good, ma'am." It's a non-answer and certainly doesn't make you enthusiastic.

Back to the conversation with the coach... I tried to get more out of him. "What do you like the most?" I tried again. "It doesn't matter, I like it all," he said. The conversation petered out.

It was totally different when I met my coach several years later. If you ask Martijn Bos what he does, he will passionately tell you how important he thinks it is to help people, and especially women, to stand up for themselves. Martijn coaches successful, female entrepreneurs in developing their mental, physical and emotional strength. He's coached me for three years now and I have become a stronger person in all respects. I recognized myself in his client profile, and because of his specialization I instantly believed he would be good at his job. He sees pitfalls and challenges before I do, knows what I will face in my process and prepares me for these in our sessions.

Customers want to work with experts in a particular area. They want to be helped by the best of the best. Be sure you're that expert.

Customers want their real question addressed

Customers will only know that you can really help when you address their question or problem. To be able to do that, you have to not only know what problem you solve, but also for whom you are solving it.

Let's say you are a real estate agent and you appeal to your clients' life area of security/safety. Your slogan could be "Feel at home in your own home," or "The reliable realtor." But what if you deal in million-dollar mansions? Does security still the play the biggest role? Or should you be appealing to your clients' status/identity areas? Then a better slogan would be "Exclusively handling extraordinary real estate."

Objections to choosing an ideal customer

Entrepreneurs are often reluctant to choose an ideal customer. They are afraid that by reducing their target group they'll have fewer customers, they'll get bored or that they'll no longer be able to work with some of the clients they really enjoy. I often hear the following objections:

If I choose a niche, I'll reach far fewer people

Out of fear they won't have enough customers, some entrepreneurs prefer to focus on everyone. The point is, it doesn't work that way. By reducing your target audience, you will distinguish yourself from the crowd, your customer will know how to find you better and he or she will feel personally addressed. One of my American colleagues, Cindy Noelk, considered herself an "accountant for everyone." She had a good business. She made enough money to pay her bills and drive a nice car. In the training program to become a Profit First Professional she was challenged to choose a niche. She eventually chose the plumbing business. When the plumbers discovered there was an accountant who was specialized in their niche – an accountant who knew all about margins, accounting systems and purchasing organizations specific to the plumbing business – they couldn't hire her fast enough and she quickly doubled her sales and profits. Customers want to work with experts, because they provide insight other professionals simply can't.

One of the other great advantages of choosing an ideal customer is that marketing becomes so much easier. You can better target your online advertising; you know which trade magazines to advertise in and which trade shows to go to. Because you're speaking your clients' language, they feel heard and understood.

I like working in so many different industries

Another objection that entrepreneurs have to choosing a niche or ideal customer is that they're afraid it will become boring.

They love being challenged all the time and they are afraid the challenge will disappear as soon as they specialize. But, if you think about it, the challenge remains the same. You go deeper instead of wider. You know everything about your ideal customer, rather than a few things about a range of different clients. You understand your ideal client's problems and challenges. You're up on current developments in the industry. You speak the language and understand the strategy.

Finally, you make it so much easier on yourself to efficiently offer a solution. Because you are an expert in a specific industry or niche, you can solve problems faster and better than someone who has to first learn all about a client's specific question.

Am I not allowed to help everyone anymore?

"Am I not allowed to work with other customers anymore?" is an objection I often hear when I ask clients to choose the ideal customer. Of course you're allowed to. It is your business, your choices. You can work with whomever you want to. However, establishing a niche and an ideal customer helps you customize what you put in your shop window – actual or virtual – and what you have in stock. On your website and in your marketing communications – your virtual shop window – you should only focus on your ideal customer. But if someone else knocks on your door, of course you are free to take them on as a customer as well. You just make it much easier on yourself if you exclusively target your ideal customer, and you also make it easier for the ideal customer to choose you.

Add extra value and raise your price

As soon as you specialize, you provide more added value. You understand the industry, the systems used within the industry and you have the right network. You know the problems your customers will face before they do. And the more you know about your customers' field and the problems they can be confronted with, the more valuable you are. You can offer a better solution that costs you less energy, time and money it costs a competitor who works for everyone. You can earn more for less effort.

A great example of this phenomenon is an anecdote that was first told in the Netherlands almost a century ago. Here's how the story goes:

In a factory, an important machine suddenly breaks down and no one knows how to get it up and running again. At the end of his rope, the director calls a retired mechanic. The mechanic listens to the machine, takes his hammer out of his toolbox and taps the machine once in a specific spot and it springs back to life. Everyone is full of praise and the mechanic returns home satisfied. A week later, the director receives a bill for 1,000 dollars. He calls the mechanic and says he thinks the bill is a bit high, exclaiming, "You only tapped the machine once with your hammer!" The mechanic replies, "The tap cost 1 dollar, knowing *where* to tap cost 999 dollars."

As soon as you start adding more value, that value must be reflected in your price. It's a logical consequence. If my accountant only provides the required bookkeeping, it is much less valuable than when my accountant helps me increase my profits.

Find your ideal client

Your ideal customer is usually not far away. Your ideal customer is someone or some company you like to work with. Often it is someone like yourself, or a company or industry that you have a lot of experience with.

Let's do a small experiment. Imagine that your ideal customer is standing at the door. Before you open it, it is important to visualize them exactly as you want them to be. You don't have to make any concessions and you don't have to be afraid that it is irreversible; your ideal customer can change and evolve throughout the days, weeks, months and years.

Visualize your ideal customer exactly as you want them to be at this moment, standing outside your door. Who is there? Is it a man? A woman? Old? Young? Hobbies or interests? Is he or she a consumer or businessperson? If it is a businessperson, how big is the company? In which industry? What are your ideal customer's most important values? How do they treat you? How much do they pay you? What are their biggest problems? Don't make any concessions to this ideal image. You don't have to ask yourself if it is realistic; it is your image. You can visualize it however you wish. Does this image make you happy? What would it be like to target this ideal customer? Maybe through this little experiment, you have been able to get a glimpse of your ideal customer.

Do a client assessment

Another way to reveal your ideal customer is to look at your current customers. A good exercise is a customer assessment. You make an overview of all your customers in the last 12 months. By each one, indicate how many hours you have spent working with them. Then note the average hourly rate per customer and how satisfied you were with it. Then note how happy you were with each customer, whether the communication went well and whether there are opportunities for growth in the cooperation. Now you can tally up a total score per customer, identifying your top customers and your not-so-great ones. See figure 3.1 for an example.

This assessment provides you with a treasure trove of valuable information. Not only do you gain insight into your current customers, but you also identify the type of customers you want more of. Then you can focus on those ideal clients. Don't hesitate to have a conversation with customers that score low in your assessment. You can adjust your rate or services, and if it is necessary, you can part ways.

Customer	Revenue (year)	Hours (per month)	€ per hour	€ per hour (satisfaction rating)	☺☺☹	Financial	Communication	Values	...	Average score
Example A	€15.000	10	€125	9	8	8	9	9		8,6
Example B	€12.000	10	€100	8	7	7	8	8		7,6
Example C	€12.000	15	€67	6	5	5	6	6		5,6

Figure 3.1 Customer assessment (inspired by the Assessment Chart from The Pumpkin Plan *from Mike Michalowicz)*

3.3 Deliver a solution

Once you know who your ideal customer is and what their real problem is, you can design a real solution and sell it. If you sell products, this is fairly obvious. For example, you sell face cream (solution) against wrinkles (problem) to women over 40 who don't want to put garbage on their face (ideal client).

Strangely, for entrepreneurs in the service industry it is not always so logical. Service providers often sell time: an hour of a day of their time. This is a disadvantage for the customer, because he or she receives time, but not necessarily a solution to his or her problem. But it is an even bigger disadvantage to the entrepreneur: she or he isn't paid for the value that she or he delivers, but for the number of hours invested. This creates the odd situation that an entrepreneur who gets better and faster actually earns less because they are finished with the work sooner.

Another big drawback to selling hours is that hours are often completely dependent on you. If you don't work because you're sick, on vacation or go to the sauna for an afternoon, the work – and therefore the profit – is on hold.

The solution consists of a number of fixed steps.

Ideally, you design a solution that the organization (people, systems and processes) provides. This solution consists of a number of steps that each customer has to go through.

Compare it to building a house. Your house is going to be totally different than your friend's. I get that. But the steps you and your buddy are taking on the road to building your new homes are generally the same. I don't know anything about building houses, but by and large it will look something like this:

Step 1: Dream. What are your wishes and dreams? What does your new house look like in your mind?

Step 2: Architect. Have an architect draw your dream.

Step 3: Land. Look for a plot of land on which your dream house can be built.

Step 4: Money. Make sure you have the finances arranged.

Step 5: Contractor. Hire a contractor.

You can create a similar step-by-step plan for the journey your ideal customer takes to get their problems solved.

Example: the personal trainer

Let's say you're a personal trainer. Your ideal customer is a busy businessman who's at least 25 pounds overweight and has his sights set on becoming strong and lean for the summer. You can charge him by the hour, of course. You can even sell him a 12-week package, so you're sure you'll work more than just one hour with him. But ideally you sell the result: 25 pounds lighter and able to bench-press his own weight by the summer.

If this man is your ideal customer, you know what it will take to achieve this result. Of course, he'll have to go to the gym, but he's also going to have to do something with nutrition, with his mindset, and you want him to get moving on the days when he's not training with you.

Now you create a program – a program that applies not only to this specific customer, but to all your ideal customers. Since you only work with ideal customers, with just minor adjustments, all your customers can follow the same program. In this program, your ideal customer goes through a number of steps. These steps all have their own content and subgoals. Now comes the crux: *you* only have to deliver some parts of some of the steps – your organization does the rest.

For the food plan, you have a questionnaire the customer completes online which is then automatically analyzed (because you've built systems). You hire a dietician (because you have a team) to discuss the plan with your client. The client's daily activity is registered with an app (again, systems). You look at your dashboard (systems) every evening to see whether all your clients have been active enough. Have they? Then you send them a compliment (because you've created processes). Do you have the impression their exercise was limited to walking from their front door to the car and back? Then give them an accountability call!

Thanks to your well-thought-out plan and the fact you hold your customers accountable, the chances are that your customers will actually be successful. They tell their colleagues – other busy businessmen who are a bit overweight and out of shape—and that's how your business gets booming.

Because your organization takes on part of the execution, you only have to do what you do best: a few hours of personal training per week and call or message the customers if they aren't active enough. This way you can handle many more customers at the same time. The total revenue value of this plan is many times higher than the costs you invest in the software program plus hiring the dietitian and your own hours. Your organization now generates profit, rather than just your individual hours worked.

Thanks to the fact that you have sold a result instead of hours, the value to your customer is much higher. You can ask a much higher price than if you had only sold your personal training hours.

Design the steps for the solution you deliver

Now back to you. The questions that you can ask yourself are:

With which steps will my ideal customer achieve the desired result? You probably know from experience exactly what steps your customer should take. But you haven't realized that most customers are already taking those steps, and you've never consciously listed those steps. By doing so, you will discover what hidden program already exists in your work. For example, a first step with a personal trainer is taking a fitness test.

What is each step's subgoal?

For each step you want to know what the subgoal or subgoals are. What should your customer be able to do or know after they've finished each step? In the example of the personal trainer, it could be a personal fitness report.

Per step: what is the best way to deliver these subgoals?

Now it gets more interesting and profitable, because if you know what the subgoal is, you can look for the best, most efficient and most effective way to deliver it. Do you have to work with your client yourself? Or can you put a team member on it? Or – what's most efficient – can you automate the step so that it is delivered by a system or process?

The personal trainer from our example can give the client the fitness test himself and write a manual report. Although this is likely to be very personal, it takes an incredible amount of time. It's much more efficient if he automates this step. The client can fill out a standard questionnaire, do a bike test with a heart rate monitor and and determine his fat percentage on a special scale. The subgoal is achieved without the personal trainer spending half a day of his time.

Action steps

- Interview your best customer and discover what his or her real problem is. Capture their exact words – these are your marketing messages.
- Dare to choose an ideal customer.
- Design a real solution, so you can sell solutions instead of hours.

In this chapter, we worked on discovering real problems, ideal customers and real solutions. These are the ingredients that you need to create your profitable plan, but in Chapter 4, we are first going to look at your business model: how you make your money.

---

1. If you want learn more about this element, I highly recommend that you read *Clockwork: Design Your Business to Run Itself*, written by my good friend and business partner Mike Michalowicz.
2. Maslow ranked his hierarchy of human needs in a pyramid. Starting at the bottom and going upwards, there are people's physical needs, safety and security, belongingness and love needs, esteem needs – prestige and the feeling of accomplishment – and at the top, self-fulfillment. According to Maslow, people can only aspire to higher needs if the lower ones have been met.

4

BUSINESS MODELS

* * *

All you have to focus on in life is to add more value than anybody else does, and you don't have to worry about anything. Be the person who does more for others and life will be anything you want – Tony Robbins / Jim Rohn

* * *

"I just earned 600 euros, you?" We're sitting on a river in the south of France. The boys are playing in the water with their shovels and pails. I've finished reading my novel and I check my email for the first time that day. There isn't anything particularly interesting. My assistant does my mail, but I've asked her to let me know if anything interesting comes in, and I see that I've sold several online training courses. My husband looks at me with a smile, "So, we're going somewhere fancy tonight for dinner?"

We have this type of conversation regularly. During my first successful launch, I earned 17,000 euros while I was sitting in the sandbox with my kids. I texted the news to my husband and he replied by sending a picture of a 1,500-euro espresso machine.

This is our inside joke. I'm proud of how I've set up my business and my husband has fun thinking of ways to spend the money – which we usually don't go through with, by the way. We don't need a new espresso machine. And going to a fancy restaurant with two young kids is, well, just not the luxurious meal you might envision.

I haven't traded my time for money in a long time, but that I get rich while I'm asleep is of course not true. Even though I think it's funny to act like I'm earning money while I'm in the pool, I work hard for it. Just not at that moment on the riverbank or in the sandbox.

4.1 Seven business models

Thanks to the online world, it's possible to make a profit in ways other than just exchanging time or a product for money. Earning money is possible in many ways: you can rent rooms, sell ice cream, trim trees, stream music. As long as you deliver something that is needed, as long as you add value, you can earn money. The way you make a profit is your business model. Many roads lead to Rome and the right business model differs by person and company. You have to make a choice. Good business models develop into the right direction on their own.

I'll take you through several popular business models and help you on your way to making the right choice for you. The basis of every business model is that you add value. By adding value, you create something that wasn't there before and, if the result meets your ideal customer's needs, it's worth money.

Trade

A very old business model is trade: you buy a product, add a margin to cover your expenses and make a profit, and you sell it again. You can resell the product as is, like online retailers often do, or you can change or add something to it.

Imagine you sell cheese. You buy your cheese through a wholesaler. You cut the cheese into small, convenient pieces and package them to sell to consumers. You don't make the cheese; you sell something that already exists. But you do add value, because consumers aren't looking for a 10-pound block of cheese. The consumer wants four ounces. In addition, you add choice. The consumer can choose from different types of cheese when shopping with you.

They can probably even try a piece before they buy. They pay for this, too. The difference between the wholesale price and the retail price of the cheese is the margin. This margin has to cover your overhead (shop rent, personnel, cutting machine, etc.) and allow you to make a profit.

This business model is still very popular. Online retailers are often traders. We all know Amazon. Amazon doesn't produce TVs or laptops, but they add an enormous amount of value through their super-fast delivery and enormous variety. Live Helfi is a smaller Dutch online retailer where I like to buy Bulletproof coffee. Live Helfi also sells various other things like protein bars, but they don't make these themselves. They buy them for resale. The value they add for me is convenience and choice. If I buy coffee in the US rather than where I live in the Netherlands, it's cheaper, but I have to add shipping and import costs, which in the end makes it more expensive. Also, the Live Helfi website is in Dutch, the delivery time is shorter, I can buy other items at the same time as my coffee, and I can pay by direct debit instead of having to use a credit card.

Manufacturing

If you manufacture something yourself, you add even more value than when you only resell it. Your margin can –and in fact must – be higher, because it costs you more energy before the product is ready for sale. Imagine you have several dairy cows whose milk you use to make cheese. In this case you don't have to buy cheese. However, your cows need food and shelter, and the work needed to make consumer-ready cheese from milk is much more extensive than simply cutting already-produced cheese into smaller pieces. In general, you need high volume and low labor costs to make manufacturing a profitable business model. If you have one cow, then making cheese is probably more a hobby than a business. If you really want to make money by making cheese, you need a factory, personnel and a lot of customers.

In the Netherlands, there are great examples of entrepreneurs who make products themselves. For example, Elma Maaskant from Creative Cosmetics. Her search for make-up made from natural ingredients led her to decide to make and sell it herself. Elma has make-up made to her specifications and sells it to salons via her online store. As a customer of Elma's, I know that she offers dozens of colors. They all need to be developed, produced, sold, packaged and shipped. The only way to do this profitably is with a really good business model, a good strategy and large volumes. Elma says herself that it is complex: "Creative Cosmetics was only profitable after three years. You really have to have sell a lot, and think a lot about your retail price. Because you have to cover not only your purchasing costs, like in reselling, but also storage, development, insurance, etc."

Charging by the hour

If we switch from products to services, then charging an hourly rate is the most obvious business model for small entrepreneurs. You perform work for a predetermined hourly rate. Initially it seems like an attractive business model. Your overhead is low; apart from a laptop, a car and some administrative costs, you don't really need anything else, and then your revenue seems high. If you charge 80 dollars an hour and work 40 declarable hours a week, you can earn around 14,000 dollars a month. Not bad, right?

At the same time, charging by the hour is a very unattractive business model. Your income is completely dependent on your input. If you're sick, go on vacation or take a course, you don't earn anything. On top of that, it's almost impossible for most service providers to work 40 billable hours a week; you need time for business development, administration, etc. And if you retire, the business stops. The value you deliver depends entirely on you. Remember the definition of a business that I gave you before: a business is a driven and profitable organization that sells a solution for the ideal customer's real problem and delivers it in the most efficient way possible. The organization is the sum of people, systems and processes. If *you* are the whole organization, it's a very vulnerable and inefficient way to solve a problem.

One to many

At a certain point, a lot of self-employed people realize the disadvantages of charging by the hour. Then they change to the "one to many" model. For example, they decide to develop and sell instructional courses. The idea is logical: if you help 10 people at the same time, in theory you can earn 10 times as much in the same amount of time. However, other challenges arise because an educational course is a totally different product and is, therefore, answering another question. So a virtual assistant who used to build online learning environments by the hour, decides to switch to training entrepreneurs to do the same work themselves. But this new entrepreneur is solving a different problem and probably appeals to a different type of ideal customer. The customers who want to outsource building online learning environments might not have any interest in learning how to do this themselves. Also, selling courses requires a new type of marketing and sales – for example, you need a lot more customers at the same time – and training others requires new knowledge and skills. The switch to "one to many" may sound attractive but, in reality, entrepreneurs often run into many obstacles, which makes this approach far from a sure thing.

Online training courses

Many service providers consider developing and selling an online training course to be the be-all-and-end-all. You create your course once and then you can sell it tens, hundreds, thousands – in theory even millions - of times, and get rich easy. This sounds great and many entrepreneurs dream of an online business model where they work four hours a week and earn more money than they can ever spend. But if it were genuinely this simple, everyone would be rich beyond their wildest dreams! Of course there are some fantastic examples of online entrepreneurs who have succeeded with this model, but they have gotten *everything* right. They have a real solution for an ideal customer's real problem, a super effective marketing and sales funnel – the route a prospective customer takes to becoming a client (see Chapter 6) – and a stellar conversion rate. If only one of these elements isn't perfect, your online training course will be an expensive investment. Creating, developing, making your course available, marketing and sales...all these vital steps require the investment of time, energy and money. And that work never stops. To keep selling an online course, you have to keep developing and marketing it.

Now that I've completely discouraged you (wink), I'll share a few success stories. I'll begin close to home. I've developed a few complete online courses. Some barely sell, others do okay and one sells really well: my "Taxes for the self-employed in 10 minutes." This is an online course that consists of a video in which I explain how Dutch income tax for the self-employed is calculated, and there's a calculator-tool that you can use to figure out how much tax you owe in your particular situation. I've sold the course hundreds of times in the past year. There are three reasons I think it does so well:

1. It solves a real problem. Many people who are self-employed can't sleep at night because they have no idea how much tax they need to pay.

2. The training is less expensive than paying your own bookkeeper to calculate your tax for you. Therefore, the risks for the buyer are low and the benefits high because you get more than just a one-time calculation, you get the knowledge and tools to repeat it as many times as you want.

3. Satisfied customers will purchase the course again the following year if the tax laws change.

Someone else who plays the online game well is the Dutch entrepreneur Simone Levie. This mother-of-three has a million-euro company. Simone was one of the first entrepreneurs in the Netherlands who discovered the phenomenon of online training courses. Not only was she earning six figures within a few years, she has taught hundreds of others to do the same. With her program "Make Beautiful Online Programs," Simone has helped almost 2,000 people. Her strength is that she takes action. Even when things aren't perfect, she starts anyway. Additionally, she knows exactly what her target group needs. After focusing only on her program for five years, she has built a brand from it. She's not afraid to invest in marketing, her team and sales. In one year, she spent almost 200,000 euros on Facebook ads. She measures precisely how much such an ad eventually brings in. Simone does things that she knows work, and changes her approach if the numbers show something isn't working. By doing this, she helped a lot of people, was able to scale up, generated great revenue and profit, and still had time for her family.

Other international entrepreneurs who have made it online are Marie Forleo, Tim Ferris and Russell Brunson.

If you see an opportunity in the market for a completely online solution, I'd say, "Go for it!" You can be successful, and there's certainly proof, but realize that if it were simple and effortless, we'd all be millionaires.

Programs

Another interesting business model is selling your service in the form of a program: a whole set of consecutive steps that provide the solution for a problem. You don't sell customers hours, but a complete solution for their question.

Imagine you're a coach, and your client wants to become more assertive. You can sell him individual coaching sessions in which you work on his goal, or you can sell him a several-months-long program. Then you determine which parts of the program he has to complete. We covered this idea in detail in section 3.3.

A program is much more valuable to your client than when he buys individual hours. You've already given a lot of thought to what's necessary to solve your client's problems. Your knowledge and experience have been packaged into a series of well-thought-out steps. If your client goes through the steps, there's a good chance he'll reach his desired goal. You can design the program so you deliver better results with less effort. You don't need to perform each step yourself; you can have other team members be responsible for some of the program, or have it delivered through systems or processes.

For example, let's say you're an assertiveness coach who explains the same theoretical model to all your clients. You could record this explanation in a video or in an e-book. Then you can deliver this part of your program via a link or email, without having it cost you any time. The value for your customer stays the same, but because you deliver this value efficiently, there's more benefit for you.

If you organize your program so the delivery is not dependent on your personal input, you've developed a viable business model.

Example: Profit First Professionals

Let me use our own Profit First Professionals (PFPs) program as an example. Our ideal customers are modern and ambitious bookkeepers, accountants and financial experts who want to make a profit out of helping their clients – entrepreneurs, for example – build financially healthy and profitable businesses. Bookkeeping or doing taxes is the foundation, which is already in place and doesn't cost them or their customers too much money, time or energy. They're looking for tools, skills and a mindset to advise their customers in selling additional services. These tools, skills and mindset are what we offer in the Profit First Professionals program.

The program consists of a community, an online course and certification. We recorded the online lessons, which can be watched by countless customers countless times. The online lessons are completely scalable. We also have several meet-up days every year, which contribute enormously to the feeling of community among the customers, and help them build a valuable network. These days require our personal attendance but, in theory, there could be hundreds of attendees together at one of the meet-up days, making it worth our while to be there.

Additionally, all PFPs receive individual online coaching sessions. We have three coaches who deliver these sessions according to an existing protocol. This way, the quality of the coaching is ensured.

The program is the culmination of off-line and on-line activities that give an answer to our ideal customer's question "How do I help my clients reach their goals in a way that's profitable to me?" And the answer is delivered in the most ideal and efficient way.

Subscriptions

Another great business model is selling services in the form of subscriptions. In the ideal situation, someone becomes a customer for life. This is a fantastic business model, because you only have to sell someone something once and, if it works out, they'll be clients for years. Newspapers and magazines were profitable for decades from subscriptions, until the internet arrived, and news became instantaneous and free online. It became more difficult for print publishers to earn money, and many went bankrupt. Telephone providers also try to keep their customers for years, but the competition is fierce, and most consumers have discovered that you can shop around every year for a better deal, or you end up paying significantly more than you need to each month.

Service providers have also discovered the subscription model. Nowadays, website developers often couple maintenance subscriptions to their website building services. Bookkeepers also do well with this model. Not so long ago, an entrepreneur had the same bookkeeper or accountant for years, if not their entire life. The bookkeeper faithfully delivered the required services year-in and year-out. But this sector is changing rapidly, too. Entrepreneurs want more from their bookkeeper than just a correct financial history; now, they're looking for a Profit Advisor. Bookkeepers who don't evolve with the times are losing their clients one after the other.

Aartjan van Erkel is a Dutch entrepreneur with a very successful subscription model running right now. Aartjan is an internet copywriter and author of the bestsellers, *Maak ze gek!*, *Make them crazy!*, and *Verleiden op internet, Seduction on the internet*. He also created "The Lab." For a monthly fee, you get access to a brand-new masterclass each month on marketing, sales or another related subject. You follow the masterclass online, and a week or two later you get the transcript in the mail, so that you can look through it again. I've been a member since the beginning, and every month when he announces what next month's topic will be, I get excited and decide to extend my subscription another month.

Other business models

There are countless other business models. You can combine models endlessly, and there will certainly be new ones in the future. The goal of this chapter is not for you to choose a business model out of the ones I've described, but to inspire you to find smart ways to offer your customers your solution to their question.

4.2 Determining the sales price

Whatever business model you choose, you will have to determine your price. You can do this in several ways.

Cost price plus margin

Just like in trade and manufacturing, the sales price is often calculated by adding a margin on top of the cost price, to cover overhead and ensure a profit. Imagine you organize a training course; you can figure out the cost price by taking your hourly rate times the number of hours it takes you to prepare and deliver the training, plus the after-sales activities. You add the cost of the venue and materials, and you have your total cost price. You still need to add a margin to cover overhead like your laptop, bookkeeper and printer and also to cover your profit. Finally, you divide the total by the number of participants. This is a way to determine the sales price. I use the "cost price plus margin" method as part of determining my prices. It shows me the minimum I need to ask for my courses. The final price depends on more ingredients than only the costs, but it is useful as a starting point.

Working with an hourly rate isn't my preference; I'm much more in favor of selling programs where the price is based on the value for the customer (see "Value pricing" in the following section.) At the same time, I do think it's important to know the minimum you need to earn per hour to pay all your costs, salary and taxes. Many entrepreneurs – especially those just starting out – estimate their minimum hourly rate much too low. They divide their salary from when they were still working for a boss by the number of hours they want to work each week. In doing so, they forget that they have overhead costs, need to save for retirement, need time for business development and administration and a lot more. It is essential you find a reliable method to calculate your minimum hourly rate.

Value pricing

A completely different way to look at determining your price is to let go of the time aspect – i.e. how many hours you work – and focus only on the value for the customer. What does it cost the customer if they *don't* solve their problem and what financial benefit do they gain if they use your product? If you know that, then you can ask the customer to invest part of their profit in purchasing your product. A rule of thumb is that you can easily ask the customer to invest 10% of the added value your product will provide. So, if your product generates 10,000 dollars for your client, you can easily ask 1,000 dollars for it.

Naturally, there are a lot of unknown variables in this calculation. To begin with, it's not always possible to express a result in terms of money. If you have a dating site, the result can be that your customer ends up head over heels in love, but is that worth 1,000 or 100,000 dollars? If, based on your nutritional advice, your client is healthier, it could be worth a million dollars, but health is difficult, if not impossible to put a price on. Another variable is who is responsible for achieving the results. If the customer buys your product, but doesn't use it, there is no result.

Value pricing is not an easy business model, because it's difficult to determine your service's value objectively. However, I still advise you to make it part of determining your price. Ask yourself the following questions:

- What will it cost your client if the problem is not solved?
- What will your client gain if they go into business with you?

Taking these numbers into consideration will improve your pricing. Additionally, you'll be more convincing when you ask for the investment.

Market value

Finally, a product is only worth what someone is willing to pay. And whatever someone is willing to pay is dependent on many factors such as your reputation as an expert, the necessity of solving the problem, and your visibility. Some coaches ask 25 dollars an hour. Tony Robbins, who has coached Oprah Winfrey and Bill Clinton, asks one million dollars per personal journey. And you'll spend at least a year on his waiting list. Your market value increases as your reputation and the trust in you and your ability to get results increases.

Action steps

In this chapter, I've gone through various popular business models with you. Use this information to determine on a good business model for your product and decide on the price you're going to ask. You need this information for the next chapter, "Create your profitable plan."

5

CREATE YOUR PROFITABLE PLAN

* * *

A good result starts with a good plan – Femke Hogema

* * *

In 2015, my revenue increased 150% compared to 2014. That sounded fantastic. And I was proud of it until I realized what had happened to my profit. It had decreased! And yes, even with my financial know-how, I hadn't seen it coming! I too am just a regular person. In 2015, I had more revenue and less profit. My company was growing; it was the year when I started working with a team, I had an online learning environment built and had invested in business coaching. And the effect was that I had spent my extra revenue on these expenses, plus a bit more. I realized I was probably not the only business owner to earn less profit while making more revenue. Surely all growing entrepreneurs must find themselves in this situation at some point.

I had still enough profit that year to pay my salary, so I wasn't panicking, but I did start to worry about the future. I had no idea if

I was on the right path to building a profitable business or if I was digging a bottomless pit. My decreased 2015 profit was the reason, at the beginning of 2016, I created my own first profitable plan. I wrote down what I wanted to offer, what it would bring in, and what it would cost. I already knew in advance what my profit would be, as long as I carried out all my plans. My profitable plan gave me incredible insights and solved a huge problem: I wasn't lying awake at night worrying anymore.

5.1 Goals of your profitable plan

Profit is not a coincidence. You have to plan profit. Profit is the added value of your product or service, translated into dollars.

What is a profitable plan?

A profitable plan is a plan in which you determine whether you can make money with your business. It's an overview, with your plans for revenue, costs and profit for the next 12 months. It's a snapshot of the future. At a glance, you see which products and services will generate revenue, how much, what costs you'll have and how much profit you'll end up with. Additionally, a good profitable plan gives insight into how much money you'll need to reserve for taxes and how much salary you can earn.

Feasibility, focus, profit and choice

The profitable plan has four important goals:

1. You know ahead of time if your plans are financially feasible, i.e. whether you can earn enough with your dream, plan or idea.

2. The profitable plan gives you focus. You know what you'll need to do to get the results you want.

3. You work towards earning enough profit, instead of only focusing on revenue.

4. You can make the right choices and adapt if the desired effects aren't being realized.

Feasibility

This may sound obvious, but you need to determine if your plans are feasible before actually doing anything. Be honest; have you calculated this yet? And if you are one of the few who has done the calculations, did you only do it because the bank or Chamber of Commerce required you to? And have you looked at your plan since? There's a big difference between determining feasibility because it's required and using that feasibility determination to build a profitable plan and create the results you desire.

I've worked with thousands of entrepreneurs over the last ten years, and I've noticed that very few of them have determined beforehand whether their plans are financially feasible. Usually, they spend a lot of time figuring out the creative part of their idea. Entrepreneurs dedicate themselves completely to the content of their plans and being able to launch them into the world. Ask them how much money they will earn, and they can't give an answer. Some clients have literally said to me, "As long as I am doing what I'm good at, the money will follow automatically."

Part of me believes this is true. Passion and perseverance are very powerful drivers. They are motivation for an entrepreneur to create something from nothing. But often, the reality is no thought has gone into what the right price should be, what costs will be incurred in order to realize the plans, how much tax will need to be paid, and whether or not there will be enough money left over to earn a decent salary and have some reserves. I understand this.

There are only a few people who get excited and grab their calculators when they read the words "revenue," "costs" and "profit." Everyone else asks themselves if they can just skip this chapter.

For many entrepreneurs, finance is a difficult subject. Finance is complex and many entrepreneurs don't know where to start. But bear with me! A successful business starts with making a profitable plan!

"A goal without a plan is just a wish."

Focus

A plan gives focus. Without a plan, you can easily make the mistake of working out of your mailbox and social media. As soon as you open your laptop in the morning, the work starts pouring in. Others want something from you: advice, an answer, a proposal – you name it. There's always enough to do, as long as you have an internet connection.

Sometimes, an entrepreneur even earns money this way. A proposal *can* result in an order, a coffee date *can* lead to cooperation. But watch out; all these questions are rooted in another person's needs.

If you don't have a plan, you work *reactively*. You react to what others want from you. The question is whether you're working on what you really want to. Are you living your mission? Or – and this is more often the case – come December, do you have to admit that another year has gone by and you've done a whole lot of things, but either you've earned too little, or still haven't carried out your best plans or – worse yet – both things are true?

As soon as an entrepreneur works from a plan, they have focus. They know exactly what they need to do this month, this week, today, right now, in order to make their plans a reality. They work from their own goals, instead of from someone else's needs.

Profit

Profit is often forgotten about in the world of entrepreneurship. Entrepreneurs are mostly focused on revenue and not on making a profit. Thanks to your profitable plan, you'll almost immediately be more profitable, simply because you're focused and do the right things to accomplish your goals.

Choices

Having a plan gives you the information you need to make the right choices. You can compare your profitable plan to your books to see if you're on track. If business isn't going according to plan, there are a few possibilities: you discover that your plan was unrealistic, you realize that you haven't done what is necessary to make it a reality, or you find out your plan is actually not what you want. Whatever your conclusion, the combination of your plan and the numbers gives you information you can use.

Resistance to creating a profitable plan

Many entrepreneurs still have resistance to making a profitable plan. For example, they say:

"I don't know how much I'm going to sell!"

"No," I always answer. "You don't know in advance how many customers you'll have and how much you'll sell. That is not the point of the profitable plan. The point is that you've calculated beforehand whether you can earn enough money when you actually do what you have in mind. If you can't make a profit on paper, then you can't make one in real life. A customer isn't going to accidently pay you more than agreed upon." It's also important that entrepreneurs understand that the plan is not set in stone. It can be constantly adapted; it's a dynamic plan.

"I don't believe in making plans. I go with the flow."

This is a dangerous statement and can be a sign the person has their head in the sand. If you say and believe this, you're not asking much of yourself. You've given yourself the excuse that you don't need to make any profit (at least not yet), so you don't need to plan. You can't fail, because there's no goal. Do you recognize yourself in this way of thinking? If you do, it's important that you realize that, while entrepreneurship often has a certain flow to it, strategic planning is vital.

"By the time the plan's finished, it's already outdated."

Entrepreneurs who say this often believe a plan must be a pages-long type of business proposal, like they probably had to write to start their business. A profitable plan is totally different. To begin with, a profitable plan usually fits on one or two pages. Additionally, it doesn't take weeks or months to create. You can actually gain valuable insights in just half a day. And remember, it's a dynamic document. If your plans change, the numbers change too. This way, it's never outdated.

Four important criteria when making your plan

When creating your profitable plan, it's easy to get bogged down in details or negative thoughts. If you pay attention to the following four criteria when making your plan, you'll be finished within a day!

1. Everything is a concept – The plan doesn't have to be perfect. In fact, that's impossible. Your plan provides insight, and there's no need for perfection. What may help is to realize that your plan is not set in stone. Plus, it's your plan. You can always change it.

2. First the outline, then the details – If you get too caught up in details when making your plan, you'll never finish it. Plus, making it becomes torture. First determine the outline and get it on paper. The details follow later.

3. Usability over accuracy – Your profitable plan is not accounting – it doesn't have to be precisely correct. Accuracy, funnily enough, is not one of the criteria. It's much more important that you can do something with the information from your plan, than knowing everything is accurate to the last cent.

4. Insight is the most important criterion – If perfection, detail and accuracy are not criteria, what is? The answer is insight. Insight is the most important criterion when creating your plan. It's about understanding the consequences of the choices you make, in particular, the financial consequences. So, if you get stuck while making your plan, ask yourself, "what will give me sufficient insight?"

"Done is better than perfect."

5.2 Creating your profitable plan

In this section, I give you hyper-specific and practical tools to make your own profitable plan. You can find the necessary documents to download at: ProfitablePlans.com.

Plan to make your plan

A good plan is not made in between appointments on a Monday afternoon. To make a good plan, you need to set time aside. Ideally, you should reserve four to eight continuous hours to create your plan and then set aside a few more hours a few days later to finalize it.

Are you committed to making your profitable plan? Then grab your agenda now and schedule the following:

- A four to eight-hour block with the description "Make profitable plan"
- One hour, one week before you make your plan, with the description "Preparation profitable plan"
- Three to five days later, a two-hour block with the description "Finalize profitable plan"

Preparing for your profitable plan day

Beforehand have several flip chart sheets ready.

- Make sure you have small sticky notes in different colors, tape, markers and a calculator.
- Get an up-to-date financial overview, and print out your profit and loss figures from the last six months.
- Calculate the total amount of personal income you've withdrawn from your business in the last months. Don't hesitate to ask your bookkeeper for help.

- In the coming week, connect with your vision and mission: why do you do what you do, and where are you going?
- In the coming week, think about your plans. What do you want to do? How do you want to help your customers best?

Your profitable plan in seven steps

During your profitable plan day or half day, you'll go through seven steps. At the end of the day, you'll know what your plans will result in, and what you need to do to make them come true.

1. Start from your mission

Making a good plan starts with your mission and vision. Begin your profitable plan day by connecting to your mission. Take a moment to think about your "why." Do this during a short morning walk or meditation. Don't start on your plan after just getting out of heavy traffic. You need the right energy.

2. Write your services and products on sticky notes

Take different colored sticky notes and write your services and products on them, one service or product per sticky note. For example, if you're a stylist, your products might be color workshops, shopping sessions, individual styling advice and VIP days. Some entrepreneurs have only one product, others twenty.

At this stage, feel free to write down all the products that come to mind. Existing products, as well as ones you've been thinking about but haven't realized yet. Later on, you'll pare them down. However, only note products and services that make money. If you want to write a book, writing costs time, but writing itself is not a product that you can sell. The book you write can be profitable, but the book is only a product from the moment it can be sold.

3. Place the services and products on a timeline

Create a timeline on a flip chart with the months of the year from left to right. Stick your chart horizontally on the wall.

Now decide in which months you'll sell which products, and stick the sticky notes on the timeline. For products you sell every month, put 12 sticky notes on the timeline, one on each month. You might sell some products only once a year, for annual or seasonal events. Stick the corresponding sticky notes on the right month.

Jan	Feb	March	April	May	June	July	Aug	Sept	Oct	Nov	Dec

Figure 5.1 Worksheet services and products

Be sure to keep the four criteria in mind: *everything is a concept*; *first the outline, then the details*; *usability over accuracy* and *insight is the most important criterion*.

Judge the feasibility

If you see all your products and services arranged on the timeline, it usually gives you instant insights. You see right away if your plans are feasible. Some entrepreneurs notice their favorite vacation times are covered with sticky notes, so they need to adapt their plan. Or, you may have a vision for the book you want to write, which means you have to create space for the time it will take to write that book.

Other entrepreneurs get stressed just by looking at all the different products and services. They realize that all the different products and services need to be developed, promoted and sold. They know it won't be possible. This is the moment to make strategic choices. When do you want to launch which new product? Move sticky notes to different months or get rid of them completely (maybe only for this year).

4. Determine the revenue

If you have a clear picture of what you're going to sell during the coming year and you're satisfied with it, this is the moment to connect dollars to your plan. Determine per product or service what revenue you'll make. Revenue always consists of two elements: quantity and price. How many participants or customers will you have? How many programs or products are you planning to sell? And at what price? You'll have to do some estimating here. No one knows beforehand exactly how many customers they'll have. No one can predict the future with 100% accuracy. The point is not to write down what will actually happen with pinpoint precision. The point is to calculate whether your plans can be profitable so you know what you need to do to reach your financial goals.

Let's say you give a workshop every month. You know the price per participant, but you must now also estimate the number of participants. The challenge is to ignore the little voice in your head saying, "Yes, but...," "How can I make that happen?" and "What if...?" You must look at your business from a director's perspective and be realistic. "How many participants will I have?" is a question you should be able to ask yourself. And challenge yourself not to get caught up in details. Usually, you already know the answer. The difficult part is writing it down on paper, because then you're making it 'real' and you're gaining insight into the viability of your business. That can be nerve-wracking, but if you don't take this step, your profitable plan remains a mirage. Get those numbers written down. Sometimes, it helps to say to yourself, "This plan is not set in stone; I can always change it. Everything is a concept, and this is just my first draft."

As soon as you have determined how much you'll sell and the price of all your products and services, you can calculate the total revenue for the coming year. Do it, and note the amount in the last column of your worksheet.

If you find it too much work to write and calculate all the amounts by hand, you can also use Excel.

5. Determine which costs you have to incur and which you want to incur to realize your goals

The first draft of the revenue part of your plan is done, and now you're going to tackle the costs. Ask yourself the question, "Which costs do I have to incur to realize my goals, and which ones do I want to incur?" This question contains several important elements.

Which costs do I have to incur?

The first part of the question is about costs. Without costs, there's no business. Expenses are inevitable. Every entrepreneur has a computer, a telephone and a bookkeeper (or better yet, a Profit Advisor, or Profit First Professional).[1] Every entrepreneur has travel expenses, marketing costs, etc.

In addition to these, there are costs you want to incur. I love spending money. For example, I particularly like spending money on education. It's necessary that I keep learning and developing, and I'm thankful my business pays for this investment.

A good first step in calculating your costs is to look at your spending during the last six months. Some costs are repeated, unchanged; note these in your plan. Try not to be too precise. It's a waste of time to confirm whether your telephone subscription is 39 or 35 dollars a month. Just write something down. This isn't a bookkeeping task, but a plan, and it is about the big picture. If you really want to have all the numbers exactly correct, do that after you've finished your first draft. "First the outline, then the details," is an important principle to remember.

...to realize my goals?

The second part of the question deals with your goals. It's not sufficient to look at the costs you've incurred so far. You need to look ahead and determine which costs you'll need to create in order to execute all your plans. Do you need to invest in new software? Do you need to expand your team? Will your marketing costs go up? These are all important questions. In your profitable plan, note all costs that you predict you'll make. Again, don't be too precise. Estimate as well as possible for now, and you can fine tune the details later. If you get lost in the details now, you'll never finish your plan and get the information you want. If your plan is off by a few hundred dollars, even a few thousand, you'll still be able to gain valuable insight.

Once you've noted all the costs as much as possible, add these up. Note the total amount in the last column.

6. Calculate the operating profit

Subtract your predicted costs from the predicted revenue; this is how you calculate your predicted operating profit. I emphasize *operating* profit, because this isn't your true profit. Taxes need to be paid, and depending on fiscal rules, possibly your personal income needs to be paid still.

How much tax do you have to pay?

The first thing you need to know is how much tax you will have to pay based on your operating profit. Your accountant or Profit First Professional can help you with this.

How much salary can you earn from your business?

Depending on fiscal rules, your personal salary is part of the costs or will need to come out of your operating profit. If the latter is the case, you will need to decide on your salary now.

Ideally, every month you automatically earn a salary from your company. Many self-employed people do this differently, and just take what they need. In my opinion this is not smart, for several reasons.

To begin with, your business should take care of you. You're the most important employee. You innovate, take risks, and probably work the hardest of everyone. That's why your company should pay you a decent, regular salary. If that isn't possible, your business isn't viable (at least, not yet).

Additionally, it's dangerous to use your business account to pay for personal things. It's far too easy for money to disappear on lots of little things, like a coffee here and a magazine there. Entrepreneurs who claim to barely use any of their business funds for private expenses are usually shocked if they count up all the little amounts, which easily add up to hundreds and sometimes thousands of dollars every month.

Last, if you regularly take little amounts out of your business account, you create bookkeeping chaos. You lose insight, and it's impossible to manage. Decide how much salary you earn each month from your company. This is a net amount. I'll give you three ways to determine how much this amount should be (but there are a number of other methods):

1. Keep the same salary you had when you were working for a boss.

2. Calculate how much you need. Really sit down and figure out how much money you need to live. If you have a partner, do this together.

3. Imagine you had to hire someone to do your job. Ask yourself what salary they'd be paid, and pay yourself this amount.

Is your net income clear? Note it in your profitable plan. Still don't know the right amount? Then write down a net salary that feels reasonable, and calculate later if it's the right amount.

How much true profit is left?

The revenue minus the costs is the operating profit. From that, you subtract the amount you need to pay your taxes. Then, you subtract your salary. What remains is the true profit – real money that's really left over. If this amount is in the black, in principle you're on solid ground. But, if this number is in the red, you have a problem. Then you're operating at a loss, and there's work to be done.

7. Assess the feasibility of your plan and fine tune

This is the moment of truth. Now, you see whether your plans are financially feasible! If you're satisfied with both your salary and the true profit, then your profitable plan is finished. Now, you only have to execute it. If your plan has resulted in a loss, or you're making less true profit than you want to, then you still have work to do. If you can't make a profit on paper, it won't work in real life either. Your customers aren't going to pay you more by accident.

There are several things you can fine tune.

Salary

You might discover that your ideal salary is unrealistic considering the current phase of your business. In that case, you realize you need to lower your salary. If you don't want to, you need to increase the operating profit or borrow money. Those are the only two options. The operating profit can go up by increasing revenue, decreasing costs or both measures together.

Decrease costs

If the problem isn't your salary, maybe you have more costs than your business can handle right now. Go through all the costs again, and for each one, ask yourself, "Are these profitable, or necessary costs?" This is the difference:

1. *Profitable costs* are costs that ensure you'll earn more. Your profitable plan should indicate whether these costs will result in more revenue in the near future.

2. In addition to profitable costs, you also have *necessary costs*. For example, the costs of good hardware and software. You can't eliminate these costs without harming your business, but maybe they can be reduced. You need a computer and a telephone, but not the newest and most expensive models every year.

3. You also have *nice-to-have costs.* These are the costs that are, well, nice to have. Items like a lease for a luxury car, a fancy office or the best graphic designer you can find are not necessary costs. If your company can't pay for these, you need to cut them.

Increasing revenue

If your salary is correct and the costs can't be reduced, the third option is increasing your revenue. What do you need to do to raise your revenue to result in enough money? Do you need to increase your price? Or quantities? Or a combination of the two? Or maybe your entire business model needs to be changed?

Borrowing money

The fourth and last option is to borrow money. If you can't get to a profitable plan from your own resources, you'll need external sources to realize your goals. Perhaps you need to make an investment that simply can't be paid out of your own pocket. Acknowledge the facts now and begin making plans to go to the bank or look for an investor.

You should only borrow money if it is really an investment you can't pay for yourself. An investment is a one-time cost for something that will earn you money later. If your profitable plan doesn't work because your costs are structurally higher than your revenue, borrowing money is the worst thing you can do. In that case your company is using money that isn't yours. The only way to fix this situation is to eliminate costs or increase revenue. Borrowing to keep the daily business going is a recipe for disaster.

There are no other options

This is it. There are no other options. The revenue must be able to fill four jars: costs, salary, tax and profit. If you can't make the numbers work, you're starting the year with unrealistic goals. Believe me, the only things you'll end up with are sleepless nights and fights with your partner. Give yourself the gift of a profitable plan on paper before you start something that ends up being impossible.

Finalizing your profitable plan

A week after you've created your profitable plan, you still have a few hours blocked in your agenda to finalize it. This is the moment to cross your t's and dot your i's.

Put your plan in Excel

Many people like to transfer their plan to Excel. This is very useful, as Excel calculates things automatically for you. As soon as you change something, Excel recalculates, and you see the consequences immediately.

Look at your plan with fresh eyes

A few nights' sleep does wonders. You've literally created distance and, more importantly, your brain recharges at night. After a few days, take another look at your plan. You'll have new insights and recognize faulty assumptions.

Fine tune

Now is the time to dive into some details. You might want more precise numbers for some of your costs or want to confirm an estimate is accurate. Maybe you want to do some additional calculations as to whether your price is right.

Print your plan

If your plan is done (NOTE: It still doesn't need to be perfect; good is good enough!), print it and hang it on the wall. This is the basis for action because your plan is just the beginning. Only action creates results.

Import your plan in your accounting software

If your accounting software has a budget module, import your profitable plan! This way you can track your progress during the year easily.

Action steps

Completing this chapter is your action step. Do you need help? Download various (free) tools at profitableplans.com.

In this chapter, I took you through the process of creating your own profitable plan. Now, you have to execute it. That's where we'll start in the next chapter.

---

1. I train bookkeepers, accountants and financial business coaches to become Profit First Professionals/Profit Advisors. If you want, we can put you in contact with a Profit Advisor trained by Profit First Professionals, via www.profitfirstprofessionals.nl (for the Netherlands and Belgium), ProfitFirstProfessionals.de (for Germany), ProfitFirstProfessionals.com.au (for Australia), ProfitFirstProfessionals.ca (For Canada) and ProfitFirstProfessionals.com (For the USA and the rest of the world).

6

THE MARKETING AND SALES PLAN

* * *

The best way to predict the future, is to create it – Peter Drucker

* * *

More than ten years ago I had coffee with a business contact one day. At the time, I was what I would call a real "one-woman company." I was working on various projects and was charging by the hour. My contact was a true salesman. I don't remember why, but at some point he explained an important sales principle to me. Back then, I didn't really know what to do with the information, but the concept he shared resonated with me, and I didn't forget it. Five years later, I've fully embraced it: the marketing and sales funnel.

He drew a funnel on a napkin and explained to me, "This is your marketing and sales funnel." (See figure 6.1) Above the funnel are the potential customers: all the people who could possibly come into contact with your service or product. In the top section of the funnel are the leads. These are people who have shown interest in your product. Lower, in the smaller part of the funnel are the people who are seriously interested. Maybe they have requested a meeting or want a proposal. At the bottom, your customers come out of the funnel. They have successfully gone through the funnel and decided to become a customer.

All your customers go through all the phases of the funnel before becoming a customer. The most important thing is to realize that as long as you have people in all the phases of the funnel, you'll always end up with customers. I call it the "law of the funnel:" as long as the funnel is full, you'll have turnover.

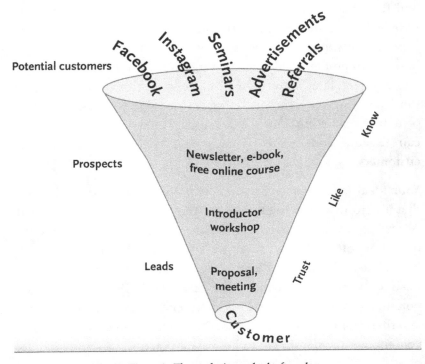

Figure 6.1 The marketing and sales funnel

Later, I discovered that this law doesn't work until after you have your first customers. Until then, you don't know whether your solution is the right answer to the customer's question. But if you have one customer, you can have ten, and if you have ten, you can have a hundred.

Thanks to your profitable plan, you know exactly when you want to sell what. Your marketing and sales activities are the "how" of your company's profitable plan. In this chapter I teach you about the sales funnel and how you, in your own way, can realize a steady flow of customers.

6.1 The sales funnel: *Know-Like-Trust*

As soon as you have a good answer (your product or service) to your ideal customer's real question and you know when, in what form and for what price you want to sell your product or service, you have arrived at the next step: introducing your product or service to others. Your product will not simply sell because it's good enough. Many entrepreneurs think marketing is difficult and sales requires being pushy. They want their product or service to sell itself, but that's not how it works. Marketing your service is an essential part of entrepreneurship. You need a good, suitable strategy that you can execute consistently. Then you'll have a steady flow of customers.

Your ideal customer needs to know your product exists, discover that it's the answer to their question and then decide to purchase it. According to the American marketeer John Jantsch, that's the definition of marketing: "Getting someone who has a need, to know, like and trust you." Everything begins with a real question, a need or problem to which you have the solution. Next, your potential customers have to know you. They have to know you exist and that your offer is exactly what they need. Then they have to like you enough to want to get to know you better. Lastly, they have to trust you. They need to have the feeling that you understand them and can help them. Every potential customer must go through these three phases, known as *Know-Like-Trust*, before becoming a customer. If you look carefully, you can see these phases in the sales funnel.

- *Potential customers*: Above your funnel you give people the opportunity to get to know you. They hear about you via social media, see your advertising, hear you speak at an event, or someone mentions you. This is the *Know* phase.

- *Prospects*: If these people get the idea that you can help them with their questions, they go from the *Know* to the *Like* phase. They aren't customers yet, but want to get to know you better. They subscribe to your newsletter, send you an email or follow your free online course. They are potential future customers: prospects.

- *Leads*: The funnel gets narrower towards the bottom. This is logical, because not everyone who has ever heard of you will end up becoming your customer. The more precisely you have defined your ideal customer, the sooner they'll feel attracted to you, and the faster they'll go to the next phase of the funnel: the *Trust* phase. This is the phase in which people trust you and show they are open to buying from you. They want to have a conversation, ask for a proposal or buy a low-threshold (i.e. low-priced) product, like an inexpensive online course or introductory workshop. They convert from prospect to lead. They're ready to take the step to buying.

- *Customers*: These are the people who eventually engage with you and to whom you offer your products. Were you successful in addressing your ideal customer's real question and have they started to trust you? Then you're well on your way to closing the deal and having a new customer.

Many salespeople – and that is what you are if you're an entrepreneur without a separate sales department – try to skip part or parts of the funnel. Last week we got a piece of paper in our mailbox: "Bob's car wash service – I'll make it shine!" I walked around with the paper in my hands for a bit. "Who is this?" I asked myself. And, "Who would actually decide to have their car cleaned based on this piece of paper?" I just got a new car, a beautiful, almost new BMW. Washing my car is not my hobby, nor one of my talents, and still I would never call the number on the paper. I don't know the person. How do I know I can trust him and that he won't use scratchy sponges on my beautiful blue car? Or won't drive away with my car and never come back? This person tried to skip all the sales funnel phases and get straight to the deal. It doesn't work like that.

I get my car cleaned at the car wash in the nearby business park. I don't know the people personally, but I know their work because my husband has his car washed there. They've been in business for years and it's a car wash with locations throughout the Netherlands, which increases my trust in them. One of my favorite things is you don't even need to get out of your car. All of this results in the fact that I know, like and trust this company. I can comfortably get my car washed there. If Bob had invested in a real flyer (his was the size of a business card, but on very thin paper,) he could have included testimonials from people in my neighborhood, or even my street, along with a photo of a sparkling clean car. If he'd made more of an effort, there would have been more chance of me trusting him and his service.

How do you make sure your ideal customer gets to know you, likes you and trusts you?

6.2 Marketing

There are literally hundreds of ways to ensure your potential customers get to know you, like you and trust you (i.e. marketing). You can be active on social media, you can sponsor the local sports team or you can blog, vlog, and speak at network events. You can advertise in trade magazines, go to trade shows or give webinars. You can create partnerships, put stickers on lampposts, or sponsor a charity. There are books and books written about every aspect of marketing. I don't claim that in half a chapter, I can tell you everything about marketing that you need to know. But I can share five important principles, and give you the tools to make your own basic marketing plan.

Five essential marketing principles

Principle 1: Don't be boring

We're are part of an information society and are bombarded with information around the clock. To keep us from going insane, we filter most of it out. We ignore information that doesn't catch our eye or seems irrelevant.

In order to be noticed by your potential customers, you have to be sure you aren't ignored. If you think of marketing as continually offering your products and services, the world will ignore you. No one is waiting around for yet more ads. Approaching marketing by telling people again and again what they can buy from you won't have much effect. You need to stand out in the overload of information that they receive. This can be achieved in many ways. I will name three.

1. Share valuable content – Share relevant information, information that actually benefits your ideal customer. For example, for years now I've always translated the Dutch government's new financial rules into what they mean for the self-employed in laymen's terms. Easy, practical tips can also be really valuable for your customer. You share your knowledge and show that you're an expert. Potential customers learn from you; they start to trust you and are curious what other wisdom you might have to share. Eventually, it's a logical next step to buy something from you. This is called content marketing. Content marketing is relatively unrelated to the channel on which you share the content. It works well if you can keep engaging with potential customers repeatedly. There are dozens of entrepreneurs who apply content marketing successfully. One of them is Elisabeth Griffioen. Elisabeth vlogs about using video to get noticed, something she does in a unique way. Elisabeth is funny and relaxed, and she shares very valuable information and tips that I can immediately put to use. I learned from her, without it costing me a penny, which gadgets I should have so that the viewer gets the impression that I'm looking directly at them. After a while, I really felt like I knew her. When I wanted to learn how to edit my videos in iMovie, I signed up for one of her courses.

2. *Get personal* – People buy from people. Potential customers will feel a bond with you sooner if they get the impression they have really connected with you and know you. That means you have to get personal. Don't just pick another successful person in your industry and try to copy their style and message. That's not personal. As soon as an article could have been written by anyone, it's less authentic, less appealing to clients who want to feel a personal connection. Strive to convey your "why" in every line of your marketing. Reveal yourself, dare to be vulnerable, and talk and write from your "why"! But remember to always keep your goal in mind. Showing vulnerability for vulnerability's sake is more pathetic than useful. That sounds harsh, but as your customer, I only benefit from your vulnerability if it's connected to a valuable lesson I need to learn.

3. *Entertain* – I have only recently become acquainted with entertainment marketing. Aartjan van Erkel (I mentioned him earlier – internet copywriter, trainer and best-selling author) was sending me great emails, day after day. I used to receive email marketing tips from Aartjan. He used content marketing. And then all of a sudden, the emails completely changed. I started getting emails about the most bizarre and varied subjects: how to light the best fire, Donald Trump's opinion on plastic straws, and how Aartjan got his baby to sleep. The crazy thing was...I read the emails. I read every single one. It was pure entertainment, a nice break during the day. I could see the little lesson hidden in every message; he would link the story to a common marketing mistake, for example. And every email ended with a call to action: an appeal to buy something. I'd followed Aartjan for years and had never bought anything from him. Within six months I bought his online course "Business Bestseller" and I became a member of "The Lab." According to Aartjan, entertainment marketing is the future. In his opinion, we've become numb from all the tips and content. Entertainment still attracts us. And I can only agree that it works.

Principle 2: Be consistent

Your ideal customer doesn't know you after only one email or Instagram story, and they won't after two either. Just like you don't get married after the first date, it takes time to build a relationship with your potential customer. This requires you to be consistent.

Don't switch communication channels every month because you're not getting immediate results. Choose one channel (or a manageable number) and persevere, even if you're not getting any response at the beginning. No response doesn't mean no one has seen your content. If you stop after only a few months because it doesn't seem to be working, or are half-heartedly active on lots of channels, all your work is for nothing.

Working on *Know-Like-Trust* takes time. Sometimes it takes years for someone to become a customer.

I remember well one time I gave a lecture on finance for the self-employed. Before I got on stage, I was drinking a cup of coffee at a standing table. A lady was already standing there and she looked at me and said, "You're Femke, right?" I almost choked on my coffee. I'd never been recognized in public before. "I've been following you for years," she said. "I've had your template to record hours ever since it started, and I still use it." This experience was a real eye-opener for me. Of course, I knew my template was popular, because I had more than a thousand downloads every year. But what I didn't realize is that there were loyal followers among the users. People who had never bought anything from me, but had been making use of my free tools for years. Then I understood I was sowing something, and, more importantly, the harvest would logically follow. By the way, the lady in question came to my Profitable Plans event for the first time last year. It took seven years, but she did become a customer.

Principle 3: Let systems work for you

If you want people to see you often, you can't avoid using systems. Target your ads so the right people see them again and again. Plan your social media posts with the available tools, so you don't have to be constantly checking and posting on Facebook or Instagram, but you still maintain an active online presence.

Create an email list, so you can email people again and again. I want to take some time to discuss this because the expression "the money is in the list" is more than true. Your list is made up of email addresses of people you have permission to contact. There's money in this list because, in addition to the content and entertainment, you also send them your offers. This is by far the easiest, and according to many, most effective way to communicate your service to people. Because the people on your list have chosen to be on it, they're literally waiting to hear from you about your products or services. It doesn't get any better than that.

Recently, I discovered firsthand how valuable it is to have a good list and how costly it can be not to. I have two email lists. My list of small entrepreneurs has almost 10,000 addresses, by Dutch standards, a respectable number. It took me more than eight years to collect them all. My other list, which I just recently started compiling, is made up of bookkeepers and accountants. There are 700 addresses on it now. I've been organizing events for years, and they're generally always full. The Profitable Plans event for entrepreneurs is sold out every year. Last year, when I held ProfitCon (a two-day seminar for bookkeepers and accountants) for the first time, I enthusiastically counted on around 150 attendees. I thought that was an easy target. This was a complete overestimate. At that moment, my mailing list of bookkeepers and accountants was around 300 addresses, and the registrations trickled in slowly. After I'd mailed everyone on the list about 10 times about ProfitCon, it became clear I wasn't going to sell any more tickets to that group. I could count the number of registrations on two hands and two feet... In the end, ProfitCon was a great success, but we didn't have 150 people there. It would have been so different if my mailing list had been 10 times bigger. It would have saved me thousands of euros on marketing and many hours of work, and we probably would have sold out.

Principle 4: Be generous

The easiest way to compile a list is to give something away for free — your "freebie" —in exchange for an email address. Good examples are an e-book, a free online course, a checklist – something digital that you only have to produce once, but can automatically give away countless times. It's important that your freebie is digital: if you give away consultations, there's a limit to the number of appointments you can manage. The process must also be completely automated. If you have to distribute freebies by hand, it costs a lot of time and energy. Once you've created your freebie, you can promote it on social media.

If your freebie is attractive enough, it will ensure your list grows quickly. It might be worthwhile to get some expert advice on the process to ensure it runs smoothly. You need an autoresponder (a system that sends emails), like an opt-in form on your website. You'll also need a link between your autoresponder and your opt-in and multiple follow-up emails. And, of course, everything must be privacy law-compliant. Setting your system up takes time, money and energy. But once it's up and running, it's a fantastic way to collect the details of potential clients who are just waiting to hear about what you have to offer!

Principle 5: Relationship building

Thanks to the internet, you can approach and engage with large groups of people simultaneously. This is great, but continuously finding new customers is labor-intensive and expensive. Keeping a customer is cheaper than finding a new one. On top of that, loyal customers are great ambassadors. There is no better gateway to a new customer than an existing customer. You don't need to focus as much energy on getting new customers if you give your existing ones plenty of attention and deliver excellent service. Do little extra things like sending cards on special occasions, call them out of the blue, or give them a gift that shows you've really thought about what makes them happy. You can turn clients into fans by doing something personal, especially as most online engagement makes real personal contact the exception rather than the rule.

6.3 Sales

Marketing is about making sure people with questions or problems get to know you, like you and trust you, so that they end up buying from you. The sale is the ultimate goal, because without sales your business can't exist. You have to close the deal. You can't close the deal without pitching it. You can make your pitch verbally – in a sales talk, during a webinar, or from a stage – but it can also be online, via an email or sales page. The best approach differs from person to person, but is mainly determined by the product or service you're selling. An inexpensive online training is usually best sold via a sales page or website. But a 10,000-dollar program will require an hour or longer personal conversation. For all the services and products you offer, you have to determine how you're going to sell them. Just like marketing, selling requires expertise. This chapter is not a complete sales training. I'm giving you an outline to help you make your plan.

The right mindset

As long as you see sales as harassing people to buy something, your business won't succeed. As long as you have a problem with selling, you'll miss a lot of opportunities *and* potential customers.

How do you feel about doing sales? What images come to mind? Are they helpful? If, when you think of sales, you only think of irritating telemarketers who ignore your "not interested" and keep going on and on about the large discount they'll give you if you buy their product, I understand if you want to avoid sales at all costs. But good salespeople don't harass people.

A few years ago, I'd requested information about a course on team coaching. My request was followed up nicely by a call from a woman, who explained the course in more detail and asked if I wanted to register. I indicated that I couldn't check my agenda right then (a euphemism for "I'm busy") and could she call back. And she did, seven times to be exact. I just couldn't decide what to do. The seventh time that she called, she said, "The course starts in two weeks. If you want to join, I need to know now." I said, "Yes," and took part in a fantastic course.

This is what is referred to as a "hard sell." Because, let's be honest, how often do you call a prospect seven times? However, I didn't experience it like that. She was simply following up, and I was the one who was hemming and hawing. Her calls were a service to me; she helped me make a decision. This is how I started to view sales. As long as someone hasn't said "yes" or "no," my role is to help them make a choice.

Whether sales is helping or harassing, there's an important difference. It becomes harassing if I ignore my customer's "no." The point is that entrepreneurs often interpret customers' reactions as "no," when they haven't actually said "no." For example, a client says, "I think it's a lot of money," or "I don't know if I have enough time," or "I'll give it some thought."

Many, many times the sales process stops there. The salesperson (that's you!) heard a "no" that wasn't there. You didn't want to harass, and stopped while your prospect hadn't actually said "no." They're just not ready to say "yes" yet. That means you have to step up your sales game. That's not harassment. It's helping.

I see sales as a process in which I help my prospect clarify their problem, and we look together whether I can and want to help solve it. If I think I'm speaking to an ideal customer and I believe I can help solve their problem, I pull out all the stops to get them to say "yes" to my offer. That means I ask questions, turn objections around and won't accept vague reactions like "I'll think about it some more." If I believe this isn't my ideal customer, then I'm the one who decides we won't be doing business.

In my opinion, a good sales conversation can only end in three ways: with a "yes," a "no," or a follow-up appointment. There's no harassment. No is no, yes is yes. And a follow-up means I know when we'll speak again. As long as a prospect doesn't make a decision, theoretically, follow-ups can continue until they do.

There's a bookkeeper I've called five times in the last two years. She keeps saying, "I really want to work with you, but I can't afford it right now." Then I ask, "When is a good moment to talk again?" The last time she said, "I think in four months." I went through my agenda and said, "Should I give you a call 10 September at 3 o'clock?" And this is how we stay in contact until there is a clear "yes" or "no."

Besides the fact that many entrepreneurs resist selling because they don't want to be pushy, there's also a lot of sales anxiety. What if the client says no?

I understand the anxiety, of course. No one likes to be rejected. And that's how it can feel if the prospect you really want to help doesn't want to be helped by you. It's helpful to disassociate your offering from yourself. There are actually three entities in the discussion: you, the prospect and your offer. You and the prospect are discussing the offer. By not coupling yourself with your offer, you're not personally being rejected if the prospect says "no" to your offer.

Likewise, it's good to disassociate yourself with your price. Entrepreneurs sometimes find it difficult to name their price, because they have the feeling it's too high, and couple it with themselves. "Am I worth it?" is their fear or hesitation.

You remove the emotion when you take the time to think about your price. If you do the calculation and, with your profitable plan, you know the price is right, you can see that right price separately from yourself. It's the price of your product or service; it has nothing to do with your value as a person.

I always teach my clients: it's your responsibility to make an offer and name your price; it's the responsibility of your prospect to either accept it or not.

Problem, desire, obstacle and source of help

In Chapter 3, I explained that you need to sell your solution and not products or processes. It's important you realize this as soon as you go to close the deal. You're not selling a course on stress management, you're selling the result, i.e. being relaxed.

You can only sell the result once you know your ideal customer has *that* problem, longs for the result you're selling, is facing obstacles you can remove, and that your solution is the best one for their problem. Whether you close the deal verbally or in writing, before someone can say "yes" to your offer, the four aspects of the question need to be addressed: the problem, the desire, the obstacle and the source of help.

Problem

The problem or the question with which your customer is struggling needs to be named. The prospect needs to have the feeling that you understand exactly what their problem is, and they need to feel it's a real problem.

This means that with every sale, there must be a connection to the problem – what's not right, is going wrong or doesn't work? If you're selling in person, you can just ask, "What's wrong?" or "What's not working?"

If you're selling in writing, then you need to specify the problem as clearly as possible in the words of your customer. You know this will only work if you truly understand the problem your ideal customer is wrestling with. Use their words. If you're a personal trainer, maybe your ideal client has an unhealthy lifestyle. I expect those aren't their words though. They would say they're "not fit" or "overweight."

Desire

Additionally, it's really important that your prospect gains insight into where they want to go, what they want to achieve and what's possible. You need to understand their desire, their longing, which goes further than merely getting rid of the problem. In a personal sales call, you can offer your customer incredible value if you help them determine what it is they really want. Try to formulate their goal so it is SMART (Specific, Measurable, Achievable, Relevant, Time-specific) as much as possible.

Personally, I use an acronym that I've added a few criteria to. Make your goal PRISMAA: Positive, Realistic, one you can Influence, Specific, Measurable, Acceptable and As-if now. I explain the elements of Prismaa in Chapter 7.

If your client wants to be fit, what does that mean for them? Is losing weight sufficient? Or do they want to be able to take the stairs without gasping for air? Play with their kids? Or finally make that days-long hike through the Grand Canyon?

Obstacle

If it's clear where your customer wants to be and where they are now, you need to understand what the obstacles are that are preventing them from reaching their goal. Why haven't they achieved what they want to? It's only in this phase that you can discover whether you can help the customer. If your customer is overweight because they don't know which foods are healthy, it's a different problem than if they overeat to deal with emotional issues or can't exercise due to major surgery.

Source of help

The fourth ingredient is the source of help: the solution. This is the way to overcome the obstacle and get from point A to point B. Ideally, this is your product. Only when the customer has connected with the problem, their desire and the obstacle, and only when you believe you can help them deal with the obstacles, can you take the step to making your offer: your service. If you're in personal contact with the customer, then summarize the problem, the desire and the obstacle, so you can then make the natural link to your offer. You can simply say, "I really want to help you get [desire] by conquering [obstacle] and solving [problem]. I've developed [solution] for this. Does that sound interesting?"

Closing the deal

Sometimes you close the deal straight away. You name the investment, and the customer agrees to work with you. It's important that you acknowledge this moment, for example by thanking the customer for their trust, congratulating them with their decision, or with a handshake, whether digitally or in person.

It's essential to take the next step immediately upon closing the deal. Grab your agenda and make the next appointment right away, or explain what will happen in the coming weeks. Once you and your client have started your journey together, you greatly reduce the risk of your client backing out of the deal.

Sometimes, you can't seal the deal. At that moment, realize that the conversations with this prospect have produced valuable insights. The chance is they've understood the value of your service, but it just might not be the right one for them. Always end the conversation positively. That way, you increase the likelihood that they'll contact you again, or refer you to a colleague with the same problem. Thank them for their openness, and ask if you could do anything else for them, refer them to one of your colleagues, or wish them all the best with their next steps. But never feel personally rejected, and don't spoil the relationship.

Often, you can't close the deal immediately, but there isn't a direct "no." Usually, there are objections. You have to manage these.

Managing objections

As soon as you've made your offer and asked for a "go," objections tend to surface. That's fine, as it only means you haven't reached the finish line yet. Your offer isn't the right solution (at least not yet), or the prospect doesn't have enough trust in you to say "yes." It's important you don't get discouraged, but that you address the objection in order to get to the core of the prospect's doubts. Usually, you'll still be able to close the deal. A win-win situation, because you have a customer, and the customer has a solution to their problem!

A difficult issue with objections is that the *real* objection often isn't what surfaces. The prospect might say, "I need to think about it," but what they mean is, "I think it's much too expensive." People tend to choose the easy way out, and it's simply more difficult to say something is too expensive than to ask for time to think. Sometimes, people don't know why they're saying "no." But their gut feeling is telling them to, so they use objections like "too expensive," "no time," or, "I need to discuss it with my partner." If you throw in the towel now, all the time and energy you've invested in the prospect will have been a waste. You owe it to yourself and to the prospect to keep asking questions, look for the real reason. Then you can get a clear "yes" or "no."

How do you do that, get to the real reason? There are basically three essential steps, which are abbreviated LSA: Listen, Summarize and Ask questions. To begin with, really listen to what the prospect is saying, objectively and without taking it personally. This is not always easy.

Acknowledge what the prospect is saying, so they feel they're really being heard. This is exceedingly important. An objection remains an objection if it isn't heard. Let's say your customer says, "I can't pay for it." If you're caught up in your own story, you'll probably argue that it's not too expensive. You say the prospect will quickly earn their investment back or, compared to similar programs, it isn't too expensive. The prospect won't feel heard, and will never ever listen to your arguments. On the other hand, if you acknowledge their issue, you show understanding and create room to keep the conversation going. For example, by saying, "I understand that it's a lot of money," you're summarizing a valid concern while keeping the dialogue going.

Now, you have the opportunity for the A of LSA; you can keep asking. You ask, for example, "If money weren't a problem, would you be interested in my program?" Now, there's room to search for other objections or doubts. The customer might say, "Well, I already tried to solve my problem, but it didn't work." What turns out to be the real issue? The customer isn't really convinced that your program will actually solve their problem. Discuss the situation honestly, and it could turn out the money isn't actually that big an obstacle after all. Often, there is money, but the money goes to another priority. When you manage objections well, you make your program the priority.

Next to "no money," another commonly heard objection is "it's not the right time." Time is a popular objection. There is a big chance you've already heard something about time earlier in the conversation. It's expert-level listening if you acknowledge your client's time crunch in your summary by saying, "Yes, you've told me you're busy with a big project." Wham! Now, you're creating trust. You really were listening to what the other person was saying. Keep asking, "When will you have time?" or "Will you have time when you've finished the project, or is there another one starting immediately afterwards?"

The last often-heard objection I want to mention is "I have to discuss it," or "I want to think about it." Your prospect is actually saying, "I don't want to say yes or no now." And personally, I think that's very smart. That's why I always say something like, "I think it's very wise that you want to take the time to think about it. This isn't a decision to make quickly." An extra acknowledgement! 😌 But don't leave it at that! Keep asking, "What is it that you want to think more about?" "What exactly do you need to discuss?" You want to be sure that all other potential objections have been addressed, otherwise you're unlikely to get to that positive answer you're seeking.

Lastly, it's important that you always make a follow-up appointment. Never hang up having just said, "Well then, I'll be hearing from you," because nine times out of ten, you won't. It isn't fair to you or the customer to let things just die out. You've both put time and energy into this dialogue, and you both deserve a clear answer. So ask, "How much time do you need?" And then, "Should we talk again next Thursday at 11 a.m.? Or do you prefer 3 p.m.?"

6.4 Make your marketing and sales plan

Now, make your own marketing and sales plan. Be sure that you know what you need to do every day to reach your goals. Start with designing your funnel and then decide on your daily marketing and sales activities.

Design your funnel

At www.profitableplans.com, you can download a free empty funnel that you can print and fill in.

1. At the top of the funnel you write how your potential customers come into contact with you. Include what you already do, or what you want to do, but be realistic. It's better to do one thing really well than five things half-heartedly. A Russian saying expresses this concept perfectly: "If you run after two rabbits, you won't catch either one."

2. Ask yourself how you can make real leads out of your potential customers. Could they request something on your website, so you can collect their contact details for your mailing list? Or will you give free webinars? Or invite people to plan an appointment with you?

3. How do you make sure that a prospect becomes a bona fide lead, and how do you convert them into a customer? Do you have a sales page on your website? Do you give individual sales talks? Or do you first offer a less expensive product, so it's easier for them to take the next step and subsequently buy something more expensive?

There are many possible routes. What it's about is that you design your ideal funnel, so you can do the things you need to do in order to fill it.

Don't underestimate making a funnel. Some entrepreneurs want three funnels right away for their three different products. Don't do that. First make one working funnel, before you start on a second one at the same time. I made the same mistake by having multiple funnels simultaneously. This is fine if you're a multinational corporation with a marketing and sales team of 30 people, but it's too much to manage for one person. Considering you probably want to actually serve your customers, you can't afford to be working on your funnels 40 hours a week.

Your marketing and sales plan

When your funnel is finished, you can make your marketing and sales plan. Which activities do you need to do at each level of the funnel?

You'll have to be very specific. Which actions are needed at which moment? Remember that your funnel should always be full. As long as you always have people in your funnel, you'll end up with customers. That's the law of sales.

Knowledge is key

After some time you'll get a feeling for how much you have to put in to get a particular result, i.e. how many proposals you need to make in order to end up with one new customer, how many sales pitches you have to give to be able to make a proposal, and how many Facebook ad views you need in order to get an invite for a sales pitch. If you know your conversion rates, you can calculate backwards.

My conversion from sales pitches is quite high. If I give ten talks, I average seven new clients. I usually reject one prospect myself, and two end up deciding against my offer. In order to speak with ten prospects, I need a minimum of 40 attendees at one of my webinars. For that, I need 70 good quality leads. This way, I can calculate that for every 10 quality registrations for my webinar, I'll end up with one new customer. Go and measure how much input you need in order to get the results you want, and then you know what you need to do to achieve those results!

Action steps

Paragraph 6.4 is your action step. Download the worksheets you need for free from ProfitablePlans.com and get to work!

Finding new customers thanks to your marketing and sales plan is now a question of taking the right steps. In the next, and final chapter, I'll give you a mega useful system to do just that!

7

TAKE ACTION

* * *

Only action creates results

* * *

For the first time, next month I'll be speaking to an audience of 4,000 people. I'll say it again, because it is a number I have to let sink in: four thousand! Speaking in front of thousands of people is something I've wanted to do for years. And wow, I've made the step from around 500 to f*cking 4,000.

Some people say, "That's so cool." While others say, "What an opportunity!" and others, "Better you than me," but almost no one says, "Well done!" Even though that is actually what it's about – the "doing." For years, I've consistently done the right things to create this moment. This isn't luck or coincidence. Yes, I've spoken previously at an international congress for accountants, and someone there was impressed by my story and speaking abilities. That's why he invited me to speak at his congress in Portugal, with – one more time – 4,000 people! You could call it luck, but that this would happen is actually completely logical to me. Organizers of large conference are always looking for the best speakers. So, if I put myself out there and tell the right story, one plus one is two.

What exactly did I do to create this moment? It started with focus. Public speaking is not something that I just do on the side. My Queen Bee role[1] (the most important activities for my business) are speaking, writing and creating. Speaking is one of the most important things I focus on. In my book *The Profit Advisor* I mention that speaking in front of a group of more than a thousand people was one of my three biggest goals. This wasn't a daydream or fantasy; this was a serious goal I set for myself.

In addition, I took the right steps to become a better and better speaker. Getting good is step 1. I spoke a whole lot and very often. In my life, I think I've been on a stage at least a thousand times – in order to get better. But scoring a lot of goals with the wrong technique doesn't make you a better soccer player. So, I hired the best trainers to work with in order to become an even better speaker. Finally, I had to engage with the right target group. So, I wrote books and blogs, and made the right contacts.

I was invited to give this specific lecture in Portugal because Joao saw me speak at the EFAA (European Federation for Accountants and Auditors) Congress and believes I'll be the perfect opening keynote speaker for his event in the fall. I've spoken at the EFAA Congress before, because Martin de Bie, Innovation Director at the accountancy firm 216, introduced me to the chairman of the EFAA. I knew Martin because I introduced myself to him. I thought he would be an important business contact to have. I found him on LinkedIn and invited myself for a coffee.

Is being invited to speak in Portugal a stroke of luck? No way. It's the culmination of years of consistently taking the right action. That's what this chapter is about.

7.1 Make a 12-week plan

Your mindset can be fantastic, your plan perfect, but in the end, there's only one thing that generates results and that's action. Consistently taking the right action, that's what counts. That means that every day you have to do precisely what's necessary to reach your desired goals. What doesn't work is turning on your laptop in the morning and emptying your inbox. That's reacting to what others want from you. It's about taking the action that *you* have decided *you* need to take to create *your* success.

Another thing that doesn't work is taking out your to-do list and working through it one thing at a time. It might keep you busy, but it doesn't make you successful, just like how you won't reach your goal if you run really fast in the wrong direction. What also doesn't work is looking at the whole year's goals in your profitable plan. One year is too long. A year feels like you have all the time in the world. In January, December seems far away. There isn't enough urgency to take action if you still have months to go. Another problem with annual plans is they allow for magical thinking. You wrongly believe the world will be different in September. Then you'll have the customers you want. You're kidding yourself if you believe things will get better on their own. If it isn't possible for you to realize your goals today, they won't miraculously happen in a few months either.

What *does* work is making a specific action plan for the coming 12 weeks[2] based on what you need to achieve in the first three months in order to realize your plans. In the 12th week, you make your plan for the following 12 weeks, and so on. Twelve weeks is a manageable amount of time. It's not so long you think you have all the time in the world, which causes procrastination, but it's long enough to be able to accomplish a lot.

Grab your profitable plan and, to begin with, decide which three to five goals you want to have achieved in three months. I'll give you a few examples:

- In 12 weeks' time, I have five new clients.
- In 12 weeks' time, tickets go on sale for my event that's taking place in seven months' time.
- In 12 weeks' time, my new website is finished.
- In 12 weeks' time, my email list has grown by 250 ideal customers.
- In 12 weeks' time, I have a publisher for my book.

Criteria that your goals need to meet

Your goals must meet certain criteria in order for you to be able to work toward them. Make your goals SMART (Specific, Measurable, Achievable, Relevant, Time-bound) or, better still, PRISMAA, an acronym I invented which stands for: Positive, Realistic, ones you can Influence, Specific, Measurable, Acceptable and As if now:

Positive – Formulate all your goals positively. There's no point in writing down what you don't want, because that doesn't help guide you in the right direction. If you don't want to spend so much time on social media, that doesn't say anything about what you do want to do. So, be sure your goal is what you *do* want instead of what you don't.

Realistic – Your goals must be attainable. That's why I recommend you limit yourself to three to five goals. It is simply impossible to focus on 25 goals at the same time. Additionally, it's important to ask yourself if your individual goals are feasible. Maybe landing five new clients isn't realistic if you never found a client before and don't know where to start. Sometimes a goal of one is a great place to start.

Influence – It's important that your goals depend on factors you can actually influence. A goal like "it'll be beautiful weather the whole of summer, so I can sell a thousand ice cream cones a day" is not within your control. Just like a goal such as "the competition makes a mess of things and then I get all their customers" isn't within your scope of influence. A goal is only a good one if it can be realized through your specific actions.

Specific – Goals are often vague. They express a desire on a global level, such as "I want to increase my status as an expert." That's fine, but vague. And it doesn't give you enough direction to do the right things. You need to think deeper; how do you define expert status? What has happened during the 12 weeks if, at the end of them, you've increased your status? Did you write an article for a national magazine? Did you double your engagement on social media?

Measurable – At the end of the 12 weeks, you want to be able to determine if you've achieved your goal or not. "I have great new clients," is not measurable, while "I have five new clients that meet my criteria for my ideal clients and who can deliver an average turnover of xxx dollars," is.

Acceptable – A goal must be acceptable for yourself as well as for others. Think about your team, your family, clients and society. If your goal is to halve the costs of your team, it's probably a good financial move. However, if all efficiency measures are already taken and the work your team needs to do isn't reduced as well, then this goal is unacceptable. If a tax advisor's goal is that their clients never have to pay taxes, at first that might sound acceptable but, if achieving it involves committing fraud, then the goal is not acceptable.

As if now – It's important that you formulate your goals in the present tense, as if you have already achieved them. This works best for your brain. Feel for yourself how much more powerful "I have a publisher" is versus "I will do my best to find a publisher." You feel it, right? Describe your goal as if in 12 weeks you will have accomplished it.

Connect actions to goals

Once your three to five goals for the coming 12 weeks are clear, connect five to ten specific actions to each goal. Which action do you need to take to realize the goal? These could be recurring activities, for example daily or weekly ones. But they could just as well be one-time activities.

If you want to write a book, you have to decide which action you need to take. Is it writing every morning between 8:00 and 10:00? Or blocking two days a week in your calendar solely for writing? If you need five new customers, the action you need to take depends on your marketing and sales funnel. Is it writing and publishing an article every week? Or making three new connections on LinkedIn every day and starting a conversation with them? Or will you plan 24 new appointments within your current network? Two each week?

At ProfitablePlans.com, you can find the worksheet that I use myself to make my 12-week plans.

7.2 Now really do it

Actually doing it is not so easy...it's 9 a.m. on Monday morning, day one of week one of your first 12 weeks. You're at your desk...and now? Are you going to do what you always do? Check your mail and let yourself be snowed under by what others want from you? Or are you going to work differently and grab your 12-week plan? You know that the latter will help you to create your success. But strangely enough, it requires more energy. It's easier to react than to create. It takes discipline to work on what's most important. I'll give you a few tips.

Through discipline comes freedom

– ARISTOTLE

Make a week plan

Even climbing Mount Everest starts with one step. If one of your 12-week goals is "be ready to start ticket sales for my event," and some of the underlying actions are: make a sales page, write mailings and determine the price, it can feel like climbing a mountain! Because the actions are still too big; they're not steps, but whole legs of the journey. Therefore, ideally, you take an hour every Monday morning to create a plan for which particular steps you need to do this week, based on your 12-week plan. Every week you make a week plan. I do this on a big flip chart in my office. It looks like figure 7.1.

Monday	Tuesday	Wednesday	Thursday	Friday

This week	Next week

This quarter	Next quarter

Figure 7.1 Example of a week plan

I use colored sticky notes to make my different goals and actions visual. The advantage of sticky notes is that you can easily move them around.

Decide during your personal Monday morning meeting which actions from your 12-week plan you want to have completed in this first week. Write it on three to five sticky notes. Now, decide the underlying tasks for each action. If one action is "finish sales page" then the tasks might be:

- Write text
- Collect testimonials
- Create product, including setting the price
- Contact website designers to create layout
- Select photographs
- Have logo designed

Ideally, the tasks can be done in an hour or less. So, "write text" should be divided up into smaller subtasks:

- Text: problem
- Text: desire
- Text: obstacles
- Text: solution - event!

Decide which of these tasks should be on your calendar this week, and stick them in the right day. The other tasks you put in the "next week" block. This way, you create a week plan with specific tasks.

Work on your 12-week actions one or two blocks a day

Don't overestimate yourself. We think we can do more than is actually feasible. It's impossible to work eight hours a day on your 12-week plan. You have to answer your email, look after your customers, do your administration and eat lunch. Take this into account in your planning.

Ideally, every day, you plan one or two blocks of two hours, in which you work specifically on the actions from your 12-week plan. You'll notice that you get results at a fast pace. It's critical that you actually plan these blocks in your calendar. Your calendar shows how much time you actually have available and also forces you to make choices.

If it's not in my calendar, it won't get done

– DAVE KERPEN

Stay focused

The time has come: your first blocked hour has started. You look at your flip chart. It says: "write blog." You open Facebook to see if there are any reactions to the photo you posted yesterday. And you're gone. Before you know it, 45 minutes have passed and you haven't written a single word. As soon as you do something new, it requires energy. Scrolling on Facebook is passive and therefore requires much less energy. Your mind takes the easier route and, before you realize it, you've already clicked on the Facebook icon.

You can't write a blog if you are checking your mail and reacting to social media posts. You need to focus your attention in order to deliver good work. Avoid getting distracted during these blocked hours.

If you recognize that you're getting distracted, snap yourself back. Close your browser, open an empty Word document and start your task. This is self-discipline, and it will make you successful in the end. By the way, this is exactly why I disagree with people who say entrepreneurship is about doing what feels right and going with the flow. Of course, writing a blog can be a real flow-activity – if you love writing and once you've got the first words written. But starting a new activity is almost never really easy. It requires self-discipline.

Create the right circumstances

It helps to create the right circumstances to make it easier. Close your office door and put a "do not disturb" sign on it. Turn your phone off. If you know that your finger finds its way to the social media icons much too easily, put a social media blocker on your computer. Get the piles of paper off your desk. Tell your team and customers about your new way of working. If they know you're not available between 8.00 and 10:00, you're giving yourself uninterrupted focus-time. A great side effect of this method, is that if you call your team members, or are on social media between 8:00 and 10:00, they'll call you out for breaking your own rules. This is the way to create an environment in which distraction becomes less likely.

Knowledge is key

The proof of the pudding is in the eating. In the end, the dollars should show you whether your actions are getting you the desired results. Are you making the profit you planned? Yes? Great! Keep going, and make another profitable plan for next year. No? Analyze what went wrong. Was turnover lower than expected? Why? There's a big chance you didn't take all the actions based on your 12-week plan. And if you did and, unexpectedly, they didn't have the result you planned, you need to go back to the drawing table. In that case, your product isn't the right answer to your customers' real questions, or your busines model is wrong, or your actions weren't enough to achieve the results you want. If you can't figure it out alone, don't hesitate to look for a good coach.

If you want, we can put you in contact with a Profit Advisor trained by Profit First Professionals, via www.profitfirstprofessionals.nl (for the Netherlands and Belgium), ProfitFirstProfessionals.de (for Germany), ProfitFirstProfessionals.com.au (for Australia), ProfitFirstProfessionals.ca (For Canada) and ProfitFirstProfessionals.com (For the USA and the rest of the world).

How do you measure if you're on the right track?

You can compare your profitable plan to your bookkeeping. Your bookkeeper, accountant, or Profit First Professional can help you. Many bookkeeping programs even have the possibility to enter your profitable plan as budget. You can then create reports where the numbers you've realized are shown next to your profitable plan.

A second really good way to measure whether you're on the right track is with the help of Profit First. Profit First is a cashflow management system. You don't work with one, but with multiple bank accounts, one for each of your monetary goals (profit, salary, opex and taxes). You calculate beforehand what percentage of each dollar you receive goes into each account.

If you work with Profit First, and all your accounts are well filled every two weeks, and not emptied prematurely, you can conclude that things are going according to plan. You can pay your bills, your business provides you with a decent salary, you save for your taxes and you have some money left over: your real profit. If you don't work with Profit First yet, I recommend you do. A Profit First Professional can help you with the implementation. If your business isn't complex, you can do it yourself with the book *Profit First*.

7.3 Go and change the world…

Now that your vision and mission are clear, you've created your profitable plan, marketing and sales plan and 12-week plan, all that's left to do is to get started.

"Will I achieve all my goals?" you may ask yourself. All of a sudden, it feels like the world is at your feet. "So, if I want five new clients, I can really make it happen?" Yes, no and yes.

First, the first "yes." Yes, this is how it works. As I've said, success is not a question of luck or coincidence. It's a question of doing the right things. If you do what's needed, you will create results.

Then the "no." Because, no, there isn't a 100% guarantee. There never is in life. Life doesn't consist solely of what you create. You have to deal with circumstances. That's where the luck can come in. Right before my book was going to the printers, it looked like my keynote speech in Portugal might be cancelled. Really disappointing. And your plan isn't a mathematical formula either. Your plan was made by you, an emotional being. Maybe even though your marketing is great, no one is interested in talking with you and you wrongly estimated interest in your product. If that's the case, you need to revise your plan.

And then, the last "yes." Because I think we should end with "yes." Because what you believe in has an incredible effect on what you achieve. If you believe that you can create your own success, it has a completely different effect on your results than if you think your fate lies in the hands of the gods. Go for it. Be determined. Persevere. And create your own success!

---

1. See *Clockwork: Design Your Business to Run Itself* by Mike Michalowicz
2. See the great book *The 12-Week Year* by Brian P. Moran.

BIBLIOGRAPHY

Femke Hogema (2020), *The Profit Advisor. The new role of accountants and bookkeepers*. Oegstgeest: Amsterdam Publishers.

Femke Hogema (2018), *Financiën voor zzp'ers en andere zelfstandige ondernemers. Hoe je een financieel gezond bedrijf runt. (Finance for solopreneurs)* Culemborg: Van Duuren Management.

Byron Katie (2003), *Loving What Is. Four Questions That Can Change Your Life.*

Brian P. Moran & Michael Lennington (2013), *The 12 Week Year. Get More Done in 12 Weeks than Others Do in 12 Months.* Hoboken: John Wiley & Sons Inc.

Mike Michalowicz (2012), *The Pumpkin Plan. A simple strategy to grow a remarkable business in any field.* New York: Penguin Group.

Mike Michalowicz (2017), *Profit First: Transform Your Business from a Cash-Eating Monster to a Money-Making Machine.* New York: Portfolio Penguin.

Mike Michalowicz (2018), *Clockwork. Design Your Business to Run Itself.* New York: Penguin Group.

Mark Tigchelaar & Oscar de Bos (2020), *Focus ON / OFF. Stop the 4 concentration leaks and get more done in our distracting world.* Amsterdam: Spectrum.

ABOUT THE AUTHOR

Femke Hogema started her career as a financial controller for large international companies. She loved figures and the clarity that figures provide about a company's health. But she also saw that entrepreneurs don't like figures, controllers, bookkeepers, or accountants. Entrepreneurs find figures boring, complicated, and theoretical. She started her company, Healthy Finance, to close this gap between entrepreneurs and figures, and to help entrepreneurs get a grip on their numbers. She gave lectures and training courses, wrote the bestseller *Financiën voor zzp'ers* (*Finance for solopreneurs*) and contributed to the Dutch edition of *Profit First*. Femke makes figures fun, practical, and accessible and in the course of ten years she inspired tens of thousands of entrepreneurs to build a financially healthy and profitable business.

Since 2017, Femke has focused on training accountants and bookkeepers to become Profit Advisors (through Profit First Professionals Netherlands). She teaches accountants and bookkeepers so that they can, in turn, support entrepreneurs in growing a financially healthy and profitable business. Femke loves to teach clients to build their own profitable company which will yield more pleasure and satisfaction.

Femke was featured as financial coach in a popular TV show on National TV. In 2019 she wrote a number one bestseller *Winstgevende Plannen* (Profitable Plans). The book reached a number one position in the Dutch National Management Book Top 100 within one and a half week after publication and kept that position for 28 days.

She gives keynotes in both the Dutch and English language about The Profit Advisor, Profit First and Profitable Plans.

ACKNOWLEDGMENTS

Being an internationally published author is one of those bucket list items that almost seem too immense to actually make your bucket list. Having my second book translated in English (and German too) is therefore something that makes me both proud and humble.

It is an honor to know that entrepreneurs from all over the world get to be inspired and take steps by reading my books.

It is my name on the cover, but it is definitely not only my accomplishment. I therefore wish to express my gratitude to quite some people.

First of all: Liesbeth Heenk of Amsterdam Publishers, for your confidence and help to publish this book internationally.

Thank you Ina Boer, this was our 3rd project at Van Duuren Management. I will always be grateful for our cooperation.

Thank you Debbie Kenyon-Jackson and team from CumLingua for the excellent translation from Dutch to English. And thank you Meggan Robinson for the excellent proofread. You totally got my style! Thank you Arjen Snijder from ArjenSnijder design for the excellent cover design!

Thank you Sonja Akkies-Grilk. No books would ever be written if it wasn't for you running our companies! The same goes for the other vital team members: Maja Donker, Esther van der Meer, Miranda Straver and Patricia Scheepmaker.

Thank you Mike Michalowicz, Ron Saharyan, Benita Königbauer, Laura Elkaslassy, Lisa Campbell and all the great Profit First Professionals from all over the world for your endless support and inspiration!

And last but not least, thank you Bart Schat, Daan and Rein for being the most important people in my world.

9 789493 231245